IN DEFENSE
OF OURSELVES

IN DEFENSE
OF OURSELVES

A Rape Prevention Handbook
for Women

Linda Tschirhart Sanford
and Ann Fetter

With a Foreword by Susan Brownmiller

A DOLPHIN BOOK
Doubleday & Company, Inc.
GARDEN CITY, NEW YORK
1979

A portion of this book, *In Defense of Ourselves: A Rape Prevention Handbook for Women*, appeared in *Family Circle*, © 1978 by Linda Tschirhart Sanford and Ann Fetter.

Library of Congress Cataloging in Publication Data

Sanford, Linda Tschirhart.
   In defense of ourselves.

   (A Dolphin book)
   Includes bibliographical references.
   1. Rape—Prevention—Handbooks, manuals, etc.
2. Self-defense for women—Handbooks, manuals, etc.
I. Fetter, Ann, joint author. II. Title.
HV6558.S24   364.4

  ISBN: 0-385-13571-8
  Library of Congress Catalog Card Number 77–15169

Acknowledgments

Together we would like to thank Karen West who edited the original manuscript and has been the source of much direction and encouragement. We would also like to thank our friend, Katie Carstens, who took the first round of sample photographs and showed us what we needed for illustrations. Mary Leberg and Lorraine Pozzi provided us with additional editing and typing.

Many professional colleagues contributed to the Conditioning and Assertiveness Exercise sections. Ginny Crow, M.S.W.; Ronald Slaby, Ph.D. and Michael Rothenberg, M.D. shared their articles with us in the Media chapter. Alison Corning Clarke, M.S.W. and Janice De Lange, Ph.D. contributed to the Self-concept chapter. Cheryl Richey, D.S.W., deserves special thanks for her direction in the Assertiveness Exercises.

Four special friends read the first draft and provided important feedback: Fran Goldin, Claudia Black, Sara Theiss and Elane Schroeder.

In any endeavor like this workbook there are an array of people who give support and advice. Among those are family, friends, the Forum staff and board of directors; and colleagues in law enforcement, the media; the Anti-Rape Movement; government; academia; Feminism. Each of you know who you are, and we thank you for being there.

Many thanks to the people in the photographs: John Baylor, Mary Cunningham, Bill Forbes, Boyd Gittins, Jeannette Halverson, David Lawski, Barb and Fritz Mondau, and Karen West. Also to my neighbors whose porches, yards and bushes appear in this book.

A special mention from Linda goes to Delores Ettress—a very important person in the beginning of the Rape Prevention Forum.

Ann adds a special and respectful thanks to Bill Reuter, her karate instructor, for respecting her feeling that women *can* be strong and showing her ways to go about it.

Linda's Dedication:
For Claudia—friend, co-therapist, former
Rhododendron Queen, support, inspiration
and confidante. This one's for you.

Ann's Dedication:
For Thelma and Everett, and Karen

And together we thank the over 6,000 women
who have taken the Rape Prevention Workshop.
We have learned much from you.

Contents

Foreword

Once upon a time in another age, or so it seems, I took the train to Philadelphia to meet with an academic who had some research material for a book on rape I was struggling to bash into shape, a book that eventually bore the title *Against Our Will*. What happened on that train was probably as significant to my patterns of thought as the exchange I had later with the academic.

Sitting two rows in front of me across the aisle was a woman I judged to be in her early thirties and who was a wreck. Disheveled hair, unraveled skirt hem, tote bag slipping off her seat and contents—mirror and wallet—spilling to the floor. That sort of thing. The woman was reading a newspaper, or trying to: The pages simply would not fold into place. She gave up with a sigh, rose and worked her way up the aisle.

Oh no, I thought to myself, she is going to the snack bar and she will come back with a styrofoam cup of coffee with a little plastic cover on it. The train will lurch, she will lose her balance and the plastic cover on the styrofoam cup and half the contents inside will go flying. Don't do it, lady, don't do it.

She did it, returning to her seat with the container of coffee and a wrapped sandwich. I watched in morbid fascination as she placed the cup of coffee on the floor of the train in order to unwrap her sandwich—no, lady, no!—the train rounded a bend, the cup overturned and a river of coffee flooded the aisle. She stared helplessly and resignedly at what she had wrought.

I was witnessing a living, breathing victim personality. If I were a mugger, a thief or a rapist I would have found my mark, my target.

Victim vibrations are not mysterious. You don't need supersonic radar to pick up the signals when they are as obvious as those of the woman on the train. The victim personality lets you know that she or he can't cope.

Now consider an assailant. He is not a courageous fellow, although he likes to think that his antisocial acts are proof of masculinity. What he wants above all is a conquest, a victory, and it doesn't take much intelligence on his part to figure out which prey looks least resistant, easy.

Statistics show that the assailant population in these United States is composed, for the most part, of young men—age nineteen or even younger is a typical profile for a physical aggressor. And there is evidence that these young men break into crime, try out their wings and gain courage by knocking off the easiest targets. Stealing hub caps off cars for starters. Progressing to hit-and-run grabs of old ladies' pocketbooks. Moving on up to the rape of young women.

We have a rather serious problem here if we are female. Young men with physical aggression on their mind consider us all to be part of their target population, and for good reason. For the most part, we're slightly smaller than they are, we carry less weight and little muscle. We haven't been trained to fight. We're easily intimidated by physical violence. We've been culturally trained to cry and maybe scream, but not to holler and yell. We don't even know how to exercise the first rule of self-defense: how to get away. We're terrified of being impolite. We are ready-made victims. In *Against Our Will* I used the phrase "Femininity has trained us to lose."

This politeness business is really important. Jim Selkin, a knowledgeable psychologist who lives in Denver, has described a classic first encounter between a would-be assailant and a polite, soon-to-be victim: A young woman walking down the street is hailed by a young man in a car. The perfect lady, she approaches the car and considerately asks what he wants. He asks her where Main Street is. Since Main Street is right around the corner she is pleased to oblige and give him directions. Next he asks if she happens to have a cigarette or a match. If she is still playing hostess at this point, if she hasn't picked up the warning signals—forget it, she's on her way toward becoming a victim.

What fascinates me about this step-by-step encounter is that while the young woman is merely exercising what she thinks is politeness, her potential assailant is deftly sizing up her compliance quotient. "Come here. Tell me something. Do this for me." And later, "Don't scream. Do what I tell you and you won't get hurt."

When I was on the college lecture circuit last year I tried out a line one evening that got an enormous response, and I repeated it at every college after that. The sentence that had popped into my head was this: "Sometimes I think that women are more afraid of being impolite than they are of being raped." The wave of recognition and embarrassed laughter that always greeted that remark never ceased to amaze me.

I had many interesting revelations and encounters on the speaking circuit. One of the nicest was when I met up with Linda Sanford, one of the authors of this book, in Seattle. She was head of the Seattle Rape Prevention Forum, a self-help group she founded, and since I was in town to speak about rape it was predictable that we met. As a matter of fact, she came to the airport to welcome me to her city.

Airport meetings between people who have never seen each other before are a little tricky. Linda had a picture of me from the back of my book cover to go by, but I must say it was I who spotted her. Of all the people lined up at the gate to greet and meet their relatives and friends, the one I picked out as being from the Rape Prevention Forum—the one I *hoped* was from the Rape Prevention Forum —was the bright, alert, self-possessed young woman with the manila file folder who was eagerly scanning the faces of the passing parade. I chose correctly. It was Linda. There's something about the clear-eyed countenance of a confident feminist.

Since my travels took me to Seattle three times that year, I had plenty of time to get to know Linda's thought processes and attitudes toward rape prevention. I liked her ideas, basically because they were so close to my own. When she told me she was trying to put together a workbook for young women—and hoped to get it published—I suggested the name of a New York agent. My attitude toward unpublished material is that it's up to agents and editors to make the decision as to what's publishable—that's not my job. Linda took it from there without another bit of encouragement or aid from me, and *In Defense of Ourselves* by Linda Sanford and Ann Fetter is the result.

I like this book because it's written by young women speaking the language of young women—and it's directed toward that target population of young women who statistically stand the greatest chance of getting raped. While any woman *can* be a victim of rape, the odds favor—or disfavor, as it were—teen-age girls.

I wish I had a dollar for every time an earnest young woman stood up in the audience at the end of one of my talks and asked me specifically how she could avoid getting raped. If only the answers were as simple as 1, 2, 3. I'd better say loudly and clearly that I believe no woman can make herself perfectly rape-free in a rape-minded culture. The ultimate answer lies in ridding society of the notion that sexual aggression is a cornerstone of masculinity. However, all too many victims of rape (and victims of other kinds of abuse ranging from the psychological to the physical) need not have been victims at all. They gave off vibes that made them likely targets; they threw in the towel of defeat too easily.

In Defense of Ourselves offers sound advice on how to avoid victimization. The authors are too wise to promise that if you read this book, you'll have done your job. The chapters on self-defense make it clear that it's not enough to learn a couple of defensive maneuvers. You have to practice, practice, practice. I think the effort will be worth it.

Susan Brownmiller

PART I

Introduction

Much has been written about how women *should* respond to a potential rape. Scholarly works on the causes and history of rape are available, but there is very little to guide women from the fears they legitimately feel to the more confident attitude needed to make an effective response. There is little available material to assist a woman to evolve from her culturally conditioned responses to where she might ultimately want to be. That is the gap we hope to fill with this book.

In our minds, a major problem with most rape-prevention literature is that it treats rape as only one kind of crime to be effectively prevented with a few techniques. The philosophy of this workbook is that rape happens along a continuum. At one end is the man you know quite well who suddenly takes a turn for the worse. At the other end is the surprise attack in the middle of the night while you are asleep in your bed.

Verbal assertiveness will not work in both cases, and physical self-defense may not always be necessary. It is important to consider each potentially dangerous situation as unique. Your response, drawing on concepts and techniques you have learned from this book, will probably be different in each case.

If, after studying this workbook, your choice would be to submit to an attack rather than to defend yourself, remember that submission is a viable alternative. Understand that you did not provoke the crime; you are its victim. Being physically assaulted does not make you less of a person.

One of our society's oldest and strongest myths is that women who are raped must have wanted it. Today, when there is so much attention given to rape prevention, we must be careful not to institute a new myth—that women who are raped are stupid or incompetent. Not all rape can be prevented. We realize that many women who read this book are past victims of rape or attempted rape. We strongly believe that no woman has anything to apologize for or feel uninformed about in their response to such a situation. We firmly believe that we all do the best we possibly can at that time. You will perhaps learn some new responses or gain a different perspective from this book, but that does not mean that your response before was wrong.

The purpose of our effort is to change the reflex of fear into a reflex of action. This can be accomplished by preparation, practice and paying attention to common-sense safety guidelines. You can change your reflexes and integrate the techniques in this book into your everyday responses to the world around you. We believe you will find changes in other areas of your life—more assertiveness in daily interactions, a positive self-concept, increased physical ability.

The reader will notice that we do not recommend the use of ploys—stories, fainting or flirting with the rapist. If, in a given situation, you feel the rapist is receptive to this, follow your intuition. But remember, stories about pregnancy, venereal disease or desire for the rapist will only work if he is listening to you and believes you, and your feelings are important to him. If this kind of caring did exist, why should he be trying to rape you? And if they don't work, can you follow through with something else?

The techniques and attitudes put forth in this book are for the purpose of responding to a potential sexual assault. If you are in a public place or in a social situation and someone—anyone—begins to hassle you, it really isn't important for you to decide if this is a potential sexual assault. You don't have the time, and because of the way rapists often make their approach, you will never really know. *All* you need to know is that you don't want this to be happening to you. From that judgment alone, you have the right to respond in an assertive manner.

For hundreds of years women have been expected to be submissive, terrified and raped. We are not coming along and saying you *should* fight back. We are presenting options. Whichever techniques you decide are right for you must be cultivated within yourself. They must be practiced.

Also, we realize that the generalizations made in this book about women's backgrounds are not true for all women. But regardless of background or belief, there is at least one technique that every woman reader will find useful. In the final analysis, we are all affected by rape.

I

The Influence of Movies and Media

When I was a teen-ager, I was told the best way to learn a foreign language was to tape record the information and play it over and over again while I slept. When I woke up the next morning, the information would be permanently stored in my subconscious.

Although I have never tried that technique in my academic career, I believe that the media in America operates to some extent on that same principle. We listen to the car radio, not really paying attention to the song lyrics, but messages to the effect that our meaning in life comes only from another person, or messages about the glories of helplessness register somewhere within us. We watch television or movies for entertainment and feel they are "pretend"—not relevant to us. Yet after countless portrayals of rapists as obviously psychotic men, we become extremely afraid when we see a man with "that look" in his eye. Oddly enough, the media in America agree to a large extent on what we should know about rape. The following scenario represents the stereotypes.

Celeste is walking down the street. It is dusk. Her arms are full of grocery bags. Celery protrudes from the top of one of the bags. She is walking through her neighborhood of apartment buildings and parking lots. Children are still playing in the schoolyard. Smiling to herself, she thinks of the day she will have children of her own and begins to hum a sentimental tune.

Suddenly she hears a scuffle in the alley to her right. She stops and looks around. Convinced she is being silly, she continues to walk and hum. But suddenly there's a man in front of her. He is unshaven, his head is tilted downward, emphasizing the evil look in his eyes. His smile is half snarl, and it shows his rotting teeth. His shirt is gray-and-white striped with a number across the right pocket. His shoes are caked with mud. He holds a knife. His fly is open. He looms over Celeste—the victim.

He moves toward her, grabs her around the waist, then holds the knife to her throat and says, "Don't scream and you won't get hurt." Celeste drops her groceries to the sidewalk. She looks beautiful. Her eyes are large with fear. He snickers as she whispers, "I'll do anything you say." He forces her into the bushes. The last scene we see is his baggy pants dropping down to his mud-caked shoes.

Most of us, having few direct encounters with rapists, formulate our concept of who rapists are from scenes like this in movies or on television. The media often portray the rapist this way or as dropping out of a tree, hunched over and drooling, with big teeth and with hair all over his body. In the few portrayals where the rapist and victim know each other, the woman always secretly wants to be raped.

In *Gone with the Wind*, Rhett Butler becomes exasperated with Scarlett O'Hara's coyness. He scoops her up in his arms and storms up the majestic staircase of Tara, while Scarlett is screeching, kicking and clawing. But alas, she is just a petite, frail woman and he a dominant man. The bedroom is his destination; the music sounds impending doom. The next scene we see is Scarlett in bed the next morning, brushing her hair, looking more satisfied than she has throughout the entire movie. Her look of relief and accomplishment leads us to the conclusion that all she needed was a good rape.

The movie makers overlooked a more realistic reaction of Scarlett in this situation. If Scarlett had delivered a good jab to the nose or spiked a strong kick to the groin (which she was in a perfect position to do) Rhett would never have uttered, "Frankly, my dear, I don't give a damn," in the same deep, clear voice.

In *Dr. Zhivago*, movie makers again teach us that sexual intercourse against our will can be fun. As Rod Steiger forces himself on Julie Christie, she first tries to struggle ineffectively. But finding that is to no avail and succumbing to her deepest, darkest wishes, she gives in with a passionate embrace and not only ends up loving it, but pregnant as well.

There is little doubt in the viewer's mind that the women deserve it. Women viewing such movies, who later find themselves in similar situations, have an inherent response that tells them that they too are helpless and deserve it. We must remember that rapists see these movies too. The scenario that women secretly want to be raped and end up loving it is played out for them as well. Whenever a woman fights, pleads or struggles in a helpless, submissive manner, the rapist expects the victim to feel like the movie heroine.

In no other film genre is this theme more prevalent than in pornography. Rape is so simple. Women do not have to take time for birth-control devices or worry about whether they should or shouldn't give in. All of these decisions are mercifully made by the rapist, who leads the woman out of this dilemma and gives her what she wants anyway.

In recent times, we have seen the exploitation of "sex for our own good" taken to yet another level in child pornography. Our country has chosen to respond to this problem as a quirk, as an outrageous phenomenon out of the mainstream of our cultural beliefs. Child pornography is an extension of the ideology that promotes a male dominant/female submissive dichotomy.

As Gloria Steinem writes in the August 1977 issue of *MS.* magazine, "It is one logical, inevitable result of raising boys to believe they must control or conquer others as a measure of manhood, and producing men who may continue to believe that success or even functioning—in sex as in other areas of life—depends on subservience, surrender, or some clear tribute to their superiority."

Child pornography makes sense in a society that encourages men to fulfill their own "needs" at any cost and considers women to be incapable of determining their own destinies. In the minds of pornographers, children serve the same purpose as women. The "advantage" is that children cannot make as many demands and have even less control over what happens to them.

The victim in the media can be a child or adult woman. The circumstances of the crime are very often not an accurate presentation. The reality the media rarely portrays is that in some cities as many as one half of reporting rape victims can give the police the first and/or last name of the rapist. It actually makes little difference whether the offender is a stranger or known to the victim—women have been successfully defending themselves for centuries. We rarely read about them in newspapers or see movies about them. These women are other people's wives and mothers, even grandmothers. They look like anyone else, have dogs and cats and even go to church on Sunday. They are not biological freaks or sociopaths as we have been led to believe. A woman who successfully defends herself need not be confused by the media's portrayal of her.

Partly because of the media's presentation of "typical" or "normal" rape, dating situations that culminate in rape are perhaps the most confusing for women. This is often when women start believing the old adage that they secretly want to be raped. A woman sometimes feels that she did something to turn this perfectly nice young man into a raving maniac. Or perhaps he was not a raving maniac. Very likely, he remained a nice young man who pointed out how much money he had spent on her or how she "teased" him into his present state of arousal. It does not seem like a "real" rape. In most cases portrayed in the media, the offender and victim are strangers until that fateful moment. These stereotypes confuse the woman who has been raped by a man she knows quite well. She may doubt it even is rape. She cannot think of another name for it but doubts anyone would believe her.

The media's concept of who the victim is, is also skewed. These misconceptions permeate talk shows as well as drama. Recently, I watched a male talk-show host interview a male psychiatrist about rape. (With all of the articulate and talented women knowledgeable in the study and treatment of sexual assault, we are consistently exposed to the male medical authorities' analysis of the problem.) The host asked the doctor if women really did ask for rape. The doctor replied that women in their nineties are raped. That wasn't the first time that particular non-answer had been given in response to that question; it seems innocuous, but it's destructive in a not-so-subtle way.

The majority of rape victims are between ten and twenty-nine years old. How does that reply address their victimization? It implies that women under ninety are in a gray area of victim precipitation of the crime. But rape is totally uninvited at *any* age. We have the right and capacity to be intimate with whom we choose at any age.

We are all familiar with the myth of the beautiful victim—alone, young, single, innocent, vibrant and helpless. Actresses portray victims in this role, even though it has little to do with who many victims really are. An even greater gap exists in the presentation of the victim's response. An angry response from the victim is rarely shown. Generally, she is totally overcome with fear, which *is* realistic. It is, however, not the entire story. An important study done by the Queens Bench Foundation in San Francisco found, in comparing rape victims to attempted rape victims, that if a woman's initial response to a potential assault was anger, the rape would probably not be completed. If her first reaction was one of fear, it probably would be completed. This is *not* to say that women who react with fear are stupid, unreal or deserve to be raped. Contrary to what the media would have us believe, the study shows that varied responses do exist, and that varied responses do have varied results.

When we do see women defend themselves adequately, as Racquel Welch and her friend did so well in *Kansas City Bombers,* the woman is depicted as a cruel joke of a human being. An overenthusiastic fan approaches these two women. They are verbally assertive in telling him that they are not interested. Not being able to believe this, he persists and quickly finds himself on the parking lot concrete. In film, only Amazons and women convicts are allowed to defend themselves. Their defense is used to prove that they are unfeminine, abnormal and deserve the viewers' contempt.

Where does the responsibility for rape fall in media portrayals? Too often it falls on the woman. The provocative dress, speech, walk or general look of the victim is only the spark that starts the fire. The proverbial coals began to burn many years ago when the rapist was just a boy. In an informal study we did during the 1976–77 prime-time television season, we found that the majority of rapists in the dramas either lived with their mothers or had a great deal of contact with their mothers. These women were depicted as being nags, manipulative, seductive, often alcoholic. One of the more prevalent family dynamics in these dramas was that of the psychotic teen-ager with thick glasses who lived with his mother and had nothing better to do, so he raped women. We also looked at where the rapist's father fit into the scheme of motivation and responsibility. Generally, the father deserted the rapist and his mother when the rapist was a small child. The message usually seems to be, who could blame the father with a wife like that? Adults in our society are expected to be responsible for their own actions, except when it comes to rape. Then it is the rapist's mother who is responsible. The directors', producers' and teleplay writers' image of the rapist is an otherwise normal young man with a castrating mother, rejecting wife or girl friend, surrounded by seductive, provocative, strange women. Unable to cope, he becomes deranged and violent. The moral of the story is that if women were just better women—as mothers, wives, girl friends and potential victims—then the problem of rape would go away.

The media specifically, and society in general, provide women with a very complete list of behaviors that precipitate rape and serve as proof that they secretly wanted to be raped. We are led to feel that we said something enticing, walked in an inviting manner, wore provocative clothing, had a reputation for being easy, or perhaps kissed or expressed affection in such a manner that the man could not control his sexual impulses. Even if one or all of these behaviors are true, the woman must not forget about all of the men who have had encounters with her and decided *not* to rape her. Instead, *she* takes responsibility for the crime. We do not assign sole responsibility for crime to the victim in any legal situation other than rape. In the countless TV shows on burglary, no one asks the victim, "Didn't that feel good when your stereo got ripped off?" We do not even dare assume that *male* rape victims secretly wanted to be raped.

The alleged irreversibility of the rapist's sex drive has been greatly glorified in the media. We are taught to believe that once it gets started, nothing will stop it. Most of us envision sex-starved men, foaming at the mouth and groping at everything in sight. The fact that most rapists have stable sexual partners (marriage, girl friends, living with a woman, etc.) and that in approximately half of reported rapes (in the Seattle area) the rapist does not ejaculate leads us to believe that rape is not a crime of passion or a way to fulfill sexual needs.

Because of the way we have assigned our values in this society, the best way to humiliate a woman is to rape her. If we suddenly decided that pulling hair was the best way to humiliate a woman, then rapists would go around pulling women's hair. If we examine our most extreme forms of profanity or our most powerful insults (for example, "you son-of-a-bitch"), we find that they are sexual and directed toward women.

The sexual element so many women fear is actually more an element of violence. Women needn't feel that rapists are nice young men walking down the street, minding their own business, who suddenly see a woman and are overcome by excessive sexual desire.

The amount of bodily harm (aside from the actual rape) done to women and the use of weapons also has been highly overrated. In almost every rape depicted on television or headlined in the newspaper, the helpless victim is brutalized. We rarely see a rapist who is frightened and confused, and we rarely see a victim who is confident, angry and able to defend herself. Rapists are some of the most powerful and confident men portrayed on television.

Even in this age of activism and thorough study of the problem of rape, the media still hangs on to the stereotype of police officers as uncaring, brutal, near-rapists themselves. A woman reporting to the police may still expect a bald man with a lollipop sticking out of his mouth, asking her, "What did you do to ask for it, baby?" Another popular television portrayal of the police officer is as a young, handsome macho knight on a white horse who charges in to save the damsel in distress. In fifty-one televised minutes, he solves the case, arrests and convicts the rapist and leaves the victim heartbroken because his first love—or his police work—is his partner. If he is neither callous nor magnetic, he is paternal and indignant about the rape of the victim. His professionalism and effectiveness are supplanted by moral outrage.

While there are still real-life police who fit these stereotypes, many police officers are trained in interviewing and investigative techniques for sexual assault. They are generally hard working, committed women and men doing a difficult job. Rape crisis centers around the country report excellent working relationships with the police. Sometimes, in newspaper or television coverage, great attention is paid to mistakes made by the police or to the still insensitive police officer. Unfortunately, an especially quick and successful investigation or sensitive treatment of a victim is not given the same attention. While the original criticism was well-deserved, it is only fair and necessary that the progress and cooperation of the police be equally heralded.

A very special improvement in police procedures has been the inclusion of more policewomen on the streets and in investigative roles. When we see this extremely important development portrayed on television, it is quite another story. The policewoman is always on the brink of danger. Most criminals on television are men. As the policewoman pursues the criminal, she usually, through carelessness, finds herself in a precarious situation.

Implicit in the tension-building scenes is the threat of rape to the policewoman.

There is a good chance that her weapon, intelligence and training will mean nothing as she faces humiliation at the hands of this lesser creature. But her male partners save her. She is grateful to them and they are protective of her. Is it progress that in one show, the investigator is saved not by a man, but by one of her sister/angels? Policewomen are rarely shown in a realistic light—as talented women providing a very serious and much-needed service.

In only a few television programs have I seen the role of a rape-crisis-center advocate included. Fortunately, many counties in America have a rape-crisis center with committed, trained and sensitive volunteers to assist a victim in working through the trauma of rape or staying with her through the law-enforcement-system process if she wishes to report. The portrayal of their work is not only good drama, but it would also provide a much-needed public service in informing the community of their existence. When rape-crisis advocates are portrayed, they appear as a group of angry, unreasonable, radical Amazons. Such depictions unfairly distort the fine work of these women. Rape-crisis advocates clearly need to be presented as an integral part of the system for the rape victim. They certainly deserve as much air time as rapists.

The soap opera was one of the first types of television programs to deal with rape. While generally the depiction is more honest and less insulting than prime-time's treatment of the problem, nonetheless it is not realistic. There is one characteristic that stands out in daytime TV's treatment of rape—in response to every incident, there will be the local "together" male reciting well-known tips about asking salesmen for identification, locking windows and doors, and not living alone. This is fine, except that the soap opera rapes are usually between people who know each other, perhaps even between husband and wife. Caution has no impact on that particular type of rape. Should these women ask for their husband's I.D. or have locks secure enough to keep dates out of their homes? Not only is the portrayal of rape limited, but the advice on prevention the soap opera women receive does not impact the type of rape she experiences. Not surprisingly, millions of women are confused by the soap opera's solution to "the social rape."

Another common distortion in television's depiction of rape is the prevalence of the false report. Although the actual incidence of false reporting for rape is lower than almost any other crime in this country, it·is a major theme in the media. We discuss burglary prevention and arson prevention without ever mentioning the hefty incidence of overdeclaring on theft reports, or arson for contract. Yet we cannot seem to talk about rape for more than a few moments without dwelling on those mythical millions of revengeful, conniving women who turn in false reports on innocent men. The very few times the insurance cheater or hired arsonist does receive air time in drama, he is not treated with nearly the same amount of disdain as the rape victim who files a false report or perhaps makes a mistake in identifying the offender. The men are treated as daring and crafty, whereas the women are unbalanced and deserve contempt.

The one chorus we hear in unison in defense of violence on television is that it is real. Violence is definitely part of our culture, so therefore it should be presented on television. Not showing it is not going to make it go away. There is reason to believe that not showing gratuitous violence would have an impact on rising crime rates, but this is not the main point of critics' arguments about television violence. The crucial issue is realism in the violence that is portrayed. Violence can be shown in a manner that does not dull our sensitivities to it.

Two cases in point are television movies written by Tracy Keenan Wynn: *The Glass House* and *The Autobiography of Miss Jane Pittman*. Violence has been a very real part of the black experience in America, as well as in our penal system. Both of these movies had numerous assaults, killings, and, in one, suicide and homosexual rape. What makes these movies valuable is that the *consequences* of violence are shown. As viewers, we felt the terror of prison life and had some perception of the impact of violence on Jane Pittman's life. These movies did not gloss over the pain inflicted on victims or imply that violent situations can be resolved in less than two hours. While few people are suggesting that violence in *any* form be eradicated from the screen, the call for realistic, responsible and thought-provoking treatment is reasonable and worth our attention.

One of the most urgent areas in need of our attention is the viewing habits of our children. According to the Nielson index, the average American child will have viewed 15,000 hours of television by the time she or he graduates from high school. The child's schooling only totals 11,000 hours. Included in this 15,000-hour lesson are approximately 18,000 murders, countless rapes, assaults, burglaries and arsons. The diet of "normal" violence is rounded out with over 350,000 commercials.

What does this have to do with rape? As stated before, we learn a great deal about our roles from what we see around us. If boys see only one role in the issue of rape—as rapists—and girls always see women acting as helpless victims, they will know nothing about other responses. In general, this volume of crime without consequence or realism ingrains in us the belief that rape is just a part of normal living.

At the end of every cop show, the rapist is put in jail by the series star. Is this not showing consequence for the crime—does it not teach us that crime doesn't pay? No, it doesn't. Often the plot is presented as a chess game in process, so the felon is merely a poorer player. Because the actual crime is never shown, and the very real terror and pain this crime causes is *never* given the air time that is afforded to the all-important glamorous chase, there is no consequence of real significance. There is no long-term trauma. Very few rapists get hurt or killed in the process of the rape. Rarely is a victim able to defend herself. Such is the scenario set up for real life. It is the scenario that children see repeated countless times.

The effect on children goes beyond girls learning to be victims and boys learning that rape and murder are male behaviors. Ronald Slaby, Ph.D., in his research at the University of Washington, delineates ten lessons that can be easily extracted by any school-age child as a result of watching hours of television violence. They are:

1. Violence is rampant
2. Violence works
3. Violence is frequently rewarded
4. Violence is often justifiable
5. Violence is clean
6. Violence is often funny
7. Violence is often done just for the fun of it

8. Violence is sometimes done in new and unique ways
9. Violence is more appropriate for males than for females
10. Violence is something to be *watched, tolerated* and even *entertained by*
    (emphasis added)

The ten lessons tend to culminate, according to Dr. Slaby's research, in three general behaviors. First, the viewer can become more aggressive. Lefkowitz, Eron, Walder and Huesmann in 1972 reported their findings in a ten-year follow-up study of 460 children to the Surgeon General's Commission on the Effects of Television Violence on Children. At age nineteen, the single best predictor of juvenile delinquency offenses in boys was the amount of television violence they watched at age nine.

Second, television violence can dull the viewer's sensitivity to real-life violence. A viewer of moderate to great amounts of television violence will be much less likely to intervene to stop a violent situation, and he or she will tolerate a much higher level of violent behavior from other people. Because violence is presented as commonplace and of no real consequence (wounds that don't bleed; suffering that only lasts five minutes) it will not be taken seriously.

Third, the viewer will form unrealistic attitudes toward violence. Fifty years ago, a child reaching puberty may have never seen a murder and would have no attitude about it. A child of fourteen today has seen an estimated 11,000 murders on television, leading him to believe that it is much more of a threat to him and plays a much greater role in our society than it really does. This is perhaps the area where our ideas about rape and sexual harassment are affected most. When girls see rape so many times, and in such bizarre circumstances, it confuses their sense of what is a threat in their environment. And boys are subliminally taught that rape is just another part of life in the big city.

If violence is presented on television, there are two variables, suggested by Dr. Michael Rothenberg in the *Journal of the American Medical Association* (December 8, 1975), that could result in inhibiting aggressive behavior in the viewer. They are "reminders that the violence was morally wrong in the terms of the viewer's own ethical principles and an awareness of the bloody, painful aftermath of aggression." Certainly these two lessons are shamefully missing from what our children view on television today. These are only two lessons that are needed to counteract the effects of the ten lessons on the nobility and necessity of violence that children are exposed to today.

Much of the research has been focused on the effects that viewing violence has on children. There is reason to believe that adults are impacted in some of the same ways. In the area of rape, it will be some time before we have definitive studies. The majority of rapists fall between fifteen and twenty-five years of age, a population that has had great exposure to the conditioning of television violence. The lessons they learn about general violence or crimes against persons can easily be applied to the execution of a rape. But recently, less has been left to their imagination. They no longer need to make the transfer of attitude from assault to rape for themselves.

As there has been pressure on the broadcast industry to curtail its preoccupation with violence in the forms of murder, beatings, car crashes and blood-letting, we have seen an increase in the incidence of rape on television. Obviously, actual rapes cannot be shown. The substitute is heavy breathing, darkness, an expressed verbal threat and off-screen sound effects. This type of violence is not in violation of the new standards for violence on television. Not enough can be said about what this psychological violence does to women viewers' feelings of fear or to male viewers' sense of legitimacy about rape. And a testimony to its pervasiveness is that we often can sense the potential for a sexual assault before any on-screen clues are given. We just know what is coming next.

While the electronic media have received the most attention in review of their contribution to our violent society, they are by no means the only culprits. Nowhere is the effect of the media more insidious than in music. We are often not aware that we are listening to a song, yet the lyrics do pervade our consciousness. We learn from the songs that we feel are important to us. Myths about rape and the glory of woman as victim are very prevalent in our music.

There is quite a variety. On the one hand, we have the rock beat of "Le Roy, We Got to Get You a Woman," rhyming such alleged womanly attributes as "fun" and "dumb" to convince us gleefully that sex on demand is noble and necessary. The Billie Holiday blues songs of "My Man" and "Ain't Nobody's Business if I Do" tell us, very poignantly, the advantages of woman battering and the double standard. Pop and soul music like "Wives and Lovers" or "If You Want to Be Happy for the Rest of Your Life, Make an Ugly Woman Your Wife," warn us of men's naturally dominant and shallow nature and our responsibility to keep them happy and at home. Nowhere is this doctrine more prevalent and blatant than in hard rock (refer to any Rolling Stones song) or country Western music. The standard "Stand by Your Man" is a leader in songs that teach us over and over again, usually with style and beautiful melodies, that it is our lot to be submissive, helpless and victimized; it is in the scheme of nature.

Music affects all of us. The most obvious way is in the glorification of rape and violence in our music. Because violence has been a large part of American history, it is reflected in our music. Violence is often analogous to patriotism, bravery or productivity (the taming of the West) and therefore acceptable. In modern days we have seen music applied to violence against women as a theme in the "war between the sexes" or as an assertion of masculine qualities (as in "Under My Thumb" and "Midnight Rambler"). And as in all types of media, the prevalence of violence glorified without any consequences serves to instill in all of us a feeling of legitimacy and innateness in one person forcing his will on another.

Another problem with violence in music is that it is possibly the most attractively packaged and easily integrated form of media contribution to our ideas. We idolize our musical stars as much as movie or television stars. We will hear a song *many* more times than we will see a television program or a specific movie. Songs are sometimes beautiful haunting melodies or they are energizing uplifting tunes. Either way, they are more likely to become a part of us than print or other visual media. If a particular singer brings us a message of violence or glamorous victimization, it may become real to us. It is extremely difficult to portray the long-range effects of eternal submission or the consequences of brutal violence in song lyrics. Usually we are left with a fantastic, slick version of what the real-life event would mean.

Women have a special issue with music. As a girl, I would spend hours choosing songs for my wedding. Looking back at the lists I kept in my journals, all the songs I chose romanticized an incomplete self-concept that could only be completed by a man. The songs convinced me that the world was a basically hostile place, over which we as women had no control, and that we would finally make sense out of it all when we found a man who would, by his very presence, make every day better.

The music we have identified with has taught us to be other-oriented and to look to others to tell us who we are and how we can be happy. We have never taken into account that the other person will also have needs, and perhaps will not be there every day to make it better. The music has not taught us that we have responsibility and control over our own careers, choices of goals, or simply that we are capable of entertaining ourselves. It has taught us that romance is a necessity, and without it, we are incomplete persons still waiting to be finished.

Too many of us were finished by that mentality through very harmful experiences. The situations we found ourselves in while searching for that romance and completion were very often dangerous and unpleasant. It is this theme that adds to the confusion of the "date rape"—the adolescent victimized by a man who believes she is seeking what the music says she wants. Many of us never give up. We continue to look for this idealization of life that we have learned and continue to hear in music. We are convinced it is just a matter of time and of correcting our own inadequacy before we find that dream and can write our own song about it.

It would be unfair to say that music alone is responsible for the fact that most of us look to others for completion and protection. But it certainly has a major influence, by virtue of its acceptability and pervasiveness. The logic of the music leaves us unprotected when we have the need to defend ourselves in a potentially dangerous situation. To consider our feelings valid and act on them to someone else's disadvantage is not in any repertoire for women in song. For a very long time, we have had only the woman as half a person to identify with. Is it reasonable to expect half a person to defend herself against the heroic, omnipotent man of song?

The situation has improved in the last few years. The era of folk music concerned with protest and the future has given us a sense of something outside ourselves and those all-important relationships. Helen Reddy's rendition of "I Am Woman" has at least offered us a very important option in our identity, whether we choose to identify with it or not. The love songs I choose for my wedding will be those of artists like Barry Manilow, songs that tell me of deep love, missing people we love, and unique happiness with one person, but do not leave out the real concepts of struggle in relationships, self-doubt or the importance of having a well-developed self-concept before a couple meets. This type of music will help us consider other alternatives to the male-dominant/female-submissive culture that keeps us victims.

We have seen in the recent past that what covers a stereo album is as telling as the music inside. A tremendous amount of clearly sadistic and pornographic photography and graphics have permeated the hard-rock album releases in the last few years. A brilliant group in Los Angeles, Women Against Violence Against Women, has led the opposition to this exploitation of women—chained, beaten, generally compromised, and allegedly loving it. This type of advertising once again teaches us all that there is nothing out of the ordinary with women as victims.

Compounding the insulting image of women in the media, there is the fact that we are not portrayed enough. The combination of being portrayed less often than we should be and those few portrayals telling us we are lost, inadequate, helpless victims plays a large part in how we see ourselves. Consider the following facts gathered by the National Commission on the Observance of International Women's Year.

1. In commercial television during 1967, of the 762 characters shown in comedies, 73 per cent were male; on crime/Western/action programs 86 per cent of the characters were male; on other types of drama, 79 per cent were male; and finally, in cartoons, there was 90 per cent male representation.[1]
2. Women's dilemmas all concerned family and romance, whereas male characters' problems involved business and acquaintances.[2]
3. Women generally did not use aggressive or defensive force, but were often victims of force.[3]

Public broadcasting did not fare much better. In monitoring eighteen hours of PBS programming, the facts were:

1. Eighty-five per cent of the characters were male.
2. Eleven of the 28 programs had *no* female participants.
3. Only 4 black women were shown during the week monitored.
4. Only 4 per cent of the shows had female announcers/narrators.[4]

The printed media also offers little for us in identification with our very important role in this society. Over 75 per cent of writers in all sections of newspapers, including the "women's section" are men.[5] Except for lifestyle or women's sections, over 70 per cent of the photographs show men.[6] (This is an odd phenomenon in a country that is 51 per cent women.)

What we hear in voice-overs on commercials is important, as that voice is *the* voice of authority. Is it any surprise that in 1974, 84 per cent of the voice-overs were male?[7] It's no surprise that 75 per cent of commercials using women are for bathroom or kitchen products.[8] A more subtle, but equally telling fact, is that women are shown as product *users*, while men are portrayed demonstrating or recommending products, but not using them.[9]

The fact that 80 per cent of film roles go to men and over 98 per cent of the writing, producing and directing of film is done by men may account for the stereotyped woman as a beautiful victim who ends up loving it.[10] Clearly, women have little input for their meager representation in film. There were better days in the past. As Joan Mellen describes in her book, *Women and Their Sexuality in the New Films,* we have seen a steady degrading of the female image in film since the 1940s.

1. In the 1940s, women were shown as autonomous career women striving to achieve their aspirations (examples: Katharine Hepburn, Joan Crawford, Bette Davis and Barbara Stanwyck).
2. In the 1950s, women were shown as "simpering, dependent hysterics" or as undulating sexual manikins (example: Marilyn Monroe).
3. In the 1960s, women were shown as remaining outside the safety of marriage and finding devastating loneliness and despair (example: Karen Black).
4. In the 1970s, women in pornography are shown as lecherous whores of endless appetite and sexual ingenuity (example: Linda Lovelace).[11]

For children, viewing reality is equally skewed. A 1975 study of children's programming found:

1. On "Sesame Street," 78 per cent of the characters (including muppets) were

male; 87 per cent of the announcers/narrators were male; males were found to initiate action more often than females, and females were found in non-active roles three times more than the male characters.

2. On "Electric Company," 69 per cent of the characters were male; there were twice as many male announcers/narrators as females; action and talking roles were divided evenly between males and females.

3. Percentage of males for four other children's shows were: "Villa Alegre," 69 per cent; "Zoom," 53 per cent; "Carrascolendas," 49 per cent; and "Mr. Rogers," 74 per cent.[12]

On Saturday morning cartoons—some of the most violent programming on television—males were shown in 42 roles while females were only in 9 roles; and males were shown as being adventurous, knowledgeable, independent, aggressive, sturdy and bold as compared to females' portrayal as romantic, submissive, fragile, timid and patient.[13]

We are not suggesting that women are empty-headed sponges who absorb whatever roles are put in front of them without discrimination or consideration. However, countless studies have shown that we basically become what people around us expect of us. When we rarely see ourselves in the media, and the few times we are portrayed it is within the very limited confines of sex-role stereotyping, it is extremely difficult for us to consider other roles or responses as viable for us. Half of the air time or printed page designated to address the lives and concerns of women is only fair. If that exposure would reflect many roles for women and a quality of life that includes our capacity to be self-determined, strong and intelligent, it would only be a mirror of our everyday reality. It is not hard to understand woman's plight as eternal victim when she sees little else in the media.

On a more positive note, we have seen quality coverage and general helpfulness from most broadcast journalism. Many local news shows have had series of interviews with victims, and presented news stories on the local rape-crisis centers that have been co-operative with police in presentation of facts about specific cases. The public-service components of many stations also have been responsible for informative coverage of the general problem.

In conclusion, the constant barrage of hard-rock music, misinformation in print and on television, and the vivid depiction of the act of rape in the movies dull our senses to the brutality of this crime. For all of us, the bizarre situations shown lead us to believe that it could never happen to someone with the ordinary lives we lead. As women, we see ourselves always in the helpless victim role, and we learn that this is what is expected of us; that this is our only feasible response. By the sheer number of rapes portrayed and lack of consequences for those acts, men learn again and again that there is nothing uncommon about forcing their will on women.

II

American Etiquette

Everyday American manners often delay responding to a situation in a way that could prevent attack. It has been proven that some rapes are preceded by a social situation—dancing together, buying a drink or by a spontaneous verbal interchange—asking a personal question, asking for directions or even approaching a woman with profanity. In these circumstances, a woman may have a premonition that the situation is potentially dangerous, but she becomes confused. Social training about what is proper and ladylike teaches her not to make a scene or attract attention to herself. She may also feel that although the situation is annoying, she is being silly to consider it dangerous.

It is *not* silly to consider the situation dangerous. Actually, we do not need to expend energy deciding whether the situation is potentially dangerous or not. All we need to know is that we want the situation to stop immediately. That decision comes easily enough for most of us. Acting on that instinctual feeling is another matter entirely. None of us have escaped the social training that prevents acting in our own best interest. We have examined some of the hard-and-fast "rules" that have been ingrained in us and often prevent us from removing ourselves from unwanted situations.

Rule Number One: When Spoken to, We Must Always Acknowledge the Other Person with a Gracious Smile

Each of us has probably carried out this rule to the point of absurdity at some time in our lives. Smiling and acknowledging almost any approach has become a reflex. In larger urban areas, this may not be the case, but the rest of us will usually at least turn to look at the person who has spoken to us.

For a potential rapist, this can serve as a "pre-test" to determine how compliant he feels you will be. If he needs to expend any more effort to get your attention, he will most likely move on to someone he feels is inherently more cooperative. For any man approaching us when we do not want to be approached, our attention is needed for him to continue.

Because we do not generally consider the option of immediately ignoring an unwanted approach, we are more vulnerable. Conditioning to smiling and politeness under the most uncomfortable circumstances begins very early. As children, we are told to be polite to adults, speak to them when they speak to us, and do what they expect of us, whether we want to or not. One friend of ours, who remembers this message being particularly stressed in her home, told us, "One day on my way home from school, a man in a car stopped me to talk. This went on for days. Then he began to make sexual comments. Then he wanted me to do favors for him. I did what I thought my parents wanted me to do . . . I was polite." Good manners are not as important as your own safety.

Those many lessons in circumventing our own natural emotions and reactions go on throughout our lives. Many married women have described parties they must attend with their husbands that turn out to be unpleasant experiences. As an example, there may be a particular client or co-worker who is important to your husband's career. While you are talking with this man—perhaps he has had too much to drink—he tells you that he wonders if you look as good with that dress off as you do in it. Not wanting to insult him, make a scene or cause problems for your husband, you smile graciously and move away from him. A tough, honest and concise statement of non-compliance would be more appropriate.

There are many reasons, beyond the sheer pervasiveness of the conditioning to immediately respond pleasantly, why we feel compelled to answer or acknowledge someone when we don't want to. One of them is peer-group pressure. Recently a woman told us, after an uninvited advance in a cocktail lounge, "So many times I feel like being rude, but there is so much peer-group pressure to be polite." The resulting peer-group pressure actually benefits the persons hassling the woman. A peer group that would have you be dainty, polite and maintain the status quo—but endangered instead of being direct, outspoken and safe—is not worth considering.

Another reason for courtesy is the fear of hurting someone's feelings, especially if we are *not sure* he has harmful intentions. Historically, it has been the women's responsibility to see that no one's feelings get hurt. Although we did not initiate the contact and have no responsibility for whatever he hopes to gain from it, we still are concerned about his feelings. He totally ignores *our* feelings simply by making the approach.

Also, women do not have much experience in acting on their own feelings of danger and seeing what happens. If we do not want to stop and respond to a seemingly innocuous question or comment, the chances of our acting on that are generally slim. We have to contend with our concern for other peoples' feelings, our reflex to be polite and helpful, and a reluctance to respond to our own gut feelings. There usually seems to be something "more important" to us than our own reactions.

The alternative to this is not the other end of the continuum—where we ignore everyone with a frozen, "if looks could kill" glare. But we need to trust ourselves. We usually know immediately if we want to have a casual conversation with the man beside us on the subway or would rather read the paper or relish the time for our own thoughts. We know if we have time to stop and give someone directions or if we just have a bad premonition of the situation and need to move on. We know that we want to eat at the table alone and really don't want to share it with anyone else today. When we do choose to engage in conversation, or respond to an approach, we have a clear idea of when we want it to end, and we have the capacity to act on that.

The key is to evaluate each approach as it comes, using your own feelings and needs as the main criteria for responding or not responding, and being able to take definitive action (see the assertiveness exercises for more ideas on this). Most importantly, if you do decide to respond, *do not* consider that an irrevocable decision. When he reaches your limits, you can choose to begin ignoring him (or fight back).

Rule Number Two: We Must Always Answer a Question that Is Asked of Us

It is difficult enough to ignore a casual response or minor request. Our culture fervently believes that it is the grossest form of rudeness not to answer a question that is put to us directly.

The most direct questions, and often the most difficult to ignore, seem to happen in a bar, tavern or cocktail party situation. We believe that every woman passing adult age in America must have been, at least once, cornered in a social situation with a barrage of undesirable questions from a less-than-desirable man. He acts as if women have come to that particular bar just to meet him. It rarely occurs to some men that women go to a bar together so they can talk with each other, enjoy a change of atmosphere or just to have a drink.

When women do tell the man that they don't care for the privilege of his company, he responds with a barrage of questions, all of which seem to say, "Why don't you drop everything and give me your undivided attention?" Women often get into danger by dignifying such questions with an answer. The men are not as interested in an answer as they are in taking up our time and attention. But we remember that it's not ladylike to ignore people.

In social situations preceding rape, the man often puts the burden of rejection on the woman. While trying to gain access to her home or acquire her name and address to help his sexual assault plan, the offender uses one of three questions (maybe all three, maybe a variation):

"What's wrong with you, don't you like me?"

"What's wrong with you, don't you like men?"

And in an interracial situation, "What's wrong with you, are you a racist?"

"Don't you like short men (fat men, bald men, young men, old men)?" The variations are endless, but all of these questions effectively make the victim feel responsible for hurting someone's feelings.

The woman compensates for hurting the man's feelings by complying with his demands. In other words, we jeopardize our own safety rather than have someone we hardly know think we don't like them. Unfortunately, the result is that women are physically and emotionally brutalized to prove they do not hate all men. It can bother us if someone we will never see again thinks we are a racist. Sometimes we value ourselves so little that when someone buys us a drink or dances with us, we think they have done us a favor. We feel we "owe" them our names or phone numbers in return.

For most women it is difficult to respond:

"No, I don't like you."

"I like some men, but not all men."

"I don't have to like you just because you're of a different race." These answers and others like them discourage the continuation of his attack, yet most women feel such remarks reflect a lack in their own moral character or manners.

Compulsive answering of questions is not an instinctual or inherent behavior in human beings. Cultures exist throughout the world where it is not considered rude to choose not to answer a question. But because we have put such a priority on polite replies in our country, the barrage of questions is one of the most common techniques used by rapists in quasi-social situations. Salesmen, political zealots and even panhandlers use the rapid series of questions as a ploy to gain our attention, monopolize our time and therefore increase our investment in talking with them. At the same time, consider how many times we as women have asked questions that have been ignored by men. Teachers, parents, bosses, coworkers, boy friends or husbands do not seem to be under the same compulsion to answer our questions if they are too busy, do not know the answer or simply would rather not be bothered.

Again, it is important to consider each question you are asked against your own wishes at the moment. If you choose not to totally ignore the question, then a short response should suffice. If you honestly believe that your response, no matter how brief it is, has fulfilled your required social obligation, then it is important for you to stand by your decision and not get dragged in any further. It is crucial for you to know that there is *nothing* wrong with you. You do not want the situation to continue, and that is *all* you need to know.

Rule Number Three: We Must Not Bother Other People or Make a Scene Because We Are Uncomfortable

In general, it is not ladylike to bother anyone at any time. We are supposed to be quiet until spoken to, never intrude but basically be ready to respond to the needs of others. This rule, as strong as it is in our backgrounds, is in direct contradiction with another equally strong rule: "When in danger, do not rely on yourself . . . scream for help."

Recently, we have seen trouble with this particular set of "rules." When we do scream for help, we very often find that other people are not willing to get involved. The only realm where these two rules reconcile themselves is if we are being dragged into the bushes by a clearly psychotic ex-convict, we are supposed to yell "fire." We are taught that if we yell "help" or "rape" no one will come to our rescue. It is rarely mentioned that women yelling fire can be prosecuted for turning in false fire alarms and distracting fire equipment from a genuine fire. An additional problem with this mentality is that it teaches us to not rely first of all on our own internal resources.

It is extremely important to know people will help. Often that is the first and most effective manner of curbing an unwanted approach. But we are unsure about how to go about getting other people's attention. We do not know how to use our own resources effectively (voice, words, action) to gain their attention. Moreover, we are confused about when we are within our rights to do so. If it will work and stop the unwanted situation, then it is appropriate. That, however, is not the lesson we are all taught. Unless it is evident to all reasonable people that we are within minutes of an untimely death, we are unwilling to "make a scene."

A classic example of this confusion happened to a very tall friend of ours who was standing outside a pizza parlor with two women friends while the rest of the group was inside paying the bill. (At the time, she had four months of martial arts training.)

It was a lovely summer evening and the street was crowded. Two short, skinny and disheveled men crossed the street, walked up to her and started fondling her breasts. They mumbled something like, "Hey baby, let's go get a pizza." Stunned by the sheer audacity of their behavior, she was immobilized.

Her friends thought she knew the men (why else such familiarity), so they ignored the situation. Our friend, in a barely audible whisper, told the two men to "drop dead." When they didn't, she said softly, "Get your hands off me."

Later she explained that she was afraid to speak louder or make a scene because people passing by on the street would wonder, "Why is that tall woman beating up on those two short men?" Yet all she needed to do was speak loudly, and it would have created enough of a scene to discourage the men immediately.

All that our friend would have needed to do was to say the exact same words in a considerably more forceful voice, and it would have been extremely difficult for those men to continue hassling her. As it was, she reported that she felt she was lucky that they were so confused they were unable to take her forcibly with them.

We are even more reluctant to draw the attention of others if we are in a social situation such as a party, bar or dance. If we have been talking with the person for quite a while and he suddenly passes our limits of what we find acceptable interaction, we will be less likely to want to attract attention to ourselves. Our fear is that those around us will think that we provoked his forward behavior, and we don't want to embarrass our friends and/or hostess at a gathering.

The solution to this dilemma is fairly straightforward. If our own statements about the need to stop the situation do not work immediately, then we are well within our rights to enlist the aid of those around us to make the point perfectly clear. Soliciting help is not only effective—and often necessary—it can also serve as a future deterrent to public actions by the offender. Also, it serves as an important warning to other women who may find themselves in a similar situation with the same man.

Rule Number Four: When in Difficulty, It Is Always Wiser to Defer to the Protection and Judgment of Men

There are two obvious flaws with this tenet. First, it is men who are endangering or bothering us. It is rather like asking the fox to guard the hen house. Second, there are not always trustworthy men around to protect us.

The Rape Prevention Forum began in response to a series of campus rapes and general sexual harassment in our area. One common event was for a housebreaker known as the "Shower Peeper" to enter the women's bathroom, walk up to one of the shower stalls, calmly pull the curtain open and stare at a coed taking a shower. Needless to say, this is a terribly frightening situation. How realistic is it to call for help when you are trapped in a shower with a strange man lurking at your only exit?

Admittedly, that is a very literal application of this rule of etiquette. Yet, the rule governs a mentality that often stops us from acting in our own defense without the backup of a man. In response to this series of terrifying crimes, our local police chief declared that the solution was to be found in the organization of a male-escort system. The proposed system consisted of fraternity men sitting by a hot-line number. When they received a call from a coed, they would immediately go to her residence and take her to class, to the library or wherever she wanted to go.

Instead of putting more energy into finding the rapist(s) or into organizing a safe transportation system for women around campus, or at the very least encouraging women to travel in pairs around the campus, the authorities found the "solution" in reducing women to parcels that needed safe handling. There was no assurance whatever that the rapist(s) was not from the fraternities. Through this system, the women were more vulnerable because great numbers of men knew their residences, schedules and perhaps their phone numbers. Women had little protection from the "escorts" they were dependent on. If a woman broke away from an escort because he was behaving inappropriately, she would be alone and again vulnerable to the rapist(s). The police chief's last statement of enthusiastic support for the program was that it would give the "men a chance to meet some girls."

We have to take the problem of the victimization of women in our society into our own hands. Often we are given no advice on how to tell the protectors from the offenders. Where does that leave us as women? Basically we're alone or with each other. And that is not a bad place to be. We *do* have the talent and intelligence to take care of ourselves. We can support and protect each other by being together, watching out for each other, and generally understanding (far better than a man) what it is like to have to cope with these problems. A man who can physically defend himself is less likely to be assaulted, and furthermore, he generally has an attitude or physical size and experience that decreases his chances of being victimized. We as women, by the virtue of our status in this society, live with this problem every day. Who would better know what is needed to alleviate the problem than another woman?

Rule Number Five: Casual Touching or Suggestive Comments in Social Settings Are Meant as a Tribute to a Woman's Desirability

This is a lesson that we all have in common. How many times have we been ogled at by a group of construction workers and quickly turned off our anger by rationalizing that they were only trying to flatter us? Many of us honestly believe that men making ape noises and creating a public spectacle of themselves are exhibiting biologically controlled expressions of men's attraction to women. Because we do not always receive praise for the things we do well, including being mothers, housewives and career women, many women feel this type of attention is the only praise they will ever get.

At a large university on the West Coast in the late sixties there was a traditional celebration of "law day" on the first day of May each year. The reason for this event was to learn about and honor our country's legal system. The law students devised a ceremony to glorify jurisprudence in our society; they lined up five members from the class on each side of a narrow walkway in the center of the campus. I was very late for class one day, and as I approached this area, I noticed a large crowd. There was no expedient way to go around the crowd. I assumed it was the result of a bicycle accident or perhaps the beginning of another rally. I pushed halfway through the crowd, excusing myself as I passed each male, and finally came to a clearing. I rushed past the clearing and into the other half of the crowd. As I was excusing myself again, I heard ten numbers called out from 7.5 to 9. I asked someone what was going on. It seemed that the law students, in tribute to those of their ranks who were judges, were imitating their role by judging each woman's attractiveness, as she passed through the clearing, on a scale of 1 to 10.

I remember being pleased that I received such high scores. It was years later before I thought that it would have been reasonable for me to be angry about the presumptuousness of those men, to be annoyed at the inconvenience the prank had caused me, or simply to be offended by being treated like a cow displayed and judged for auction. And on Law Day, of all times, by men who might in the future be prosecuting rape cases!

Many people, both men and women, might think this episode was just harmless fun; boys will be boys, and where is my sense of humor? My sense of humor about such "happenings" disappeared when I began to value myself enough not to feel it necessary or even permissible to be judged in public on *any* of my numerous attributes. My sense of humor also disappeared when I learned that *many* sexual assaults begin with a "harmless" compliment or inquiry from the rapist. He has planned the crime and is setting the scenario in motion by testing how amenable his victim will be.

As she enters puberty, a young woman may be whistled at by groups of men, approached in a theater or store for lewd purposes; perhaps persuaded by an older schoolmate or her brother's friends to do something sexual with them.

Her first response might be anger at being treated like a commodity. She may not consider the men involved to be desirable and may be offended that they think they can treat her like a possession. Often, first reactions are the healthiest.

If she discusses the subject with an older, "wiser" person, she may be told that men who whistle are flattering her, that men like the guy in the theater are something all pretty girls have to contend with, and as for her brother's friends, well, boys will be boys and she should simply avoid them.

These experiences are by no means universal. But many women harbor some of these basic ideas, and the result is confusion.

Later in life when she is being pressured to go home with the man in the tavern, she may have a premonition that the situation is potentially dangerous, but on the other hand, this man is just trying to be nice and she shouldn't be rude and reject him. She has not been taught to believe *she* is a worthwhile person; thus, any man giving her his time and attention is, in her estimation, doing her a favor.

The lack of clarity about what constitutes insulting behavior, and the learned ambivalence we have about the meaning of unwanted approaches, makes us very vulnerable to sexual assault. It is not necessary to stop and explain the moral and political implications of their comments to a group of construction workers who have made reference to your breasts as you walk down the street. In that case, ignoring them and continuing to walk down the street is probably the best course of action, and you have the right to be angry. In the same way, if you are out on a date, or at a party, and a man tells you your breasts do strange things to him, it is not necessary to thank him or to continue the conversation when his comments make you uncomfortable. Taking our own feelings seriously is the first step toward having them taken seriously by society.

Rule Number Six: It Is the Natural State of Affairs for Men to Carry the Financial Burden of Social Situations

This particular rule is losing some of its strength as more women insist on paying their own way. Yet, it is still a popular rationale for men (although by no means all) to justify demanding sex.

Some of us probably remember finding this custom rather odd as girls. Girls new to dating might ask why the boy has to pay. Why doesn't the girl pay too? One answer is that he pays for her company. She might ask, "But aren't I enjoying the benefit of his company as well? Why shouldn't I pay too?" A typical response is that that's the way things are. Later the woman might learn that for some men paying for dates is their insurance for getting something beyond the pleasure of her company.

We know one man who has adapted the ploy of spending money on women in return for sexual favors to the constraints of inflation. Traditionally, a man's manipulation to sleep with a woman because he has spent a lot of money on her is quite an extravaganza (as in the "I Am Man, You Are Woman" scene between Omar Sharif and Barbra Streisand in *Funny Girl*). It includes, but is not limited to, expensive wine, exotic candlelight dinner, a romantic walk in the park, perhaps a hit play or movie, then home to his place to see his etchings. A man we know takes his dates to a buffet-type restaurant that offers all you can eat for under five dollars. The food is basic—fried chicken, lasagne, mashed potatoes. The atmosphere is well lit and crowded. He genuinely feels that the volume of food his date gets at the meal offsets the lack of planning or romantic atmosphere. He honestly believes that she owes him a sexual encounter because he bought her this meal.

This rule does not affect us so much in the area of being chosen as a victim as theme in situation comedies. There is nothing funny about reducing a woman or relationship to something that can be bought on time payments, yet we see it again and again. It is particularly confusing for younger women and for those of us who cannot pay our own way.

It is particularly important that adolescents who date have money of their own that goes beyond "mad money" (the historical dime in the bra to call the police) so that they are not so totally dependent on their dates. The autonomy and self-respect that come with not always being paid for by one's escort becomes important in reacting to potentially dangerous situations—or simply getting out of situations that one does not want to be in.

Rule Number Seven: When Engaged in a Social Encounter, It Is Improper for a Woman to Prove Herself Superior at Any Game or Sport She and Her Date Are Engaged in

This rules does not affect us so much in the area of being chosen as a victim as it affects our ability to defend ourselves. Very early, women are told that under no circumstances should they beat their dates at games, be it pool, tennis, Scrabble or Monopoly. It will hurt a man's pride and decrease his interest. (On the other hand, *his* success is supposed to enhance her interest in him.) She is supposed to feed and reinforce an ego that believes it has the right to win everything including a woman's body.

Thus, we are deprived of the training we need to protect ourselves. If we are never allowed to win at anything with a man, it is expecting a lot to ask a woman to effectively deal with someone trying to rape her.

We do know of a few cases where the rapist says he chooses "uppity" women as victims. On a more basic level, we often hear of couples who have altercations over the woman's success and the man's failure in the same endeavor. A friend of ours and her husband once went to a tavern seventy-five miles away from their home to meet with some friends and play pool. The husband prided himself on his pool shooting skill. After an evening of drinking and talking with people, the husband was annoyed because the wife was getting more attention from their friends than he was. To break up the social gathering, he suggested a pool tournament. To round off the perfect evening, his wife beat him in the first game. He was so deflated, he quietly slipped out of the tavern and drove home by himself, leaving his wife to find her own way home.

Very few of us have escaped that type of scene. The danger is having a mind set that trivializes our own resources and talents in deference to a man's. Such subservience is never justified, but it is particularly difficult to understand when our society has created these silent rules in the realm of something as non-monumental as games or sports. It can be as healthy for our social partners to see us at our best as it is for us to reach that potential. The sheer silliness of expected passivity needs to be recognized and eradicated in order for women to know they are capable of defending themselves.

Rule Number Eight: We Must Always Accept the Kindness of Strangers When They Offer to Help Us with Our Heavy Burdens

It was Blanche DuBois, in *A Street Car Named Desire*, who stated that she had always depended on the kindness of strangers. We can take a good lesson from where that got her in her relationship with Stanley Kowalski.

We tend to trust people who approach us, offer help, and seem to have our best interest at heart. In the ideal world, we could universally accept such offers as altruistic and not fear danger. Unfortunately, we do not live in an ideal world, and too often the ploy of "I'm helping you for your own good; you obviously need it" is used by potential rapists who have the crime planned well in advance. They gain the entrance to our home that they need.

For example, a woman we work with had this frightening experience. A few years ago, she lived in an apartment with her fiance in a college community. Carrying heavy packages in her arms, as she approached her apartment building, two men got out of a waiting car and took the packages from her. They carried them up to the apartment, asking her many questions about her living situation. Surprised to find a man in the apartment, they asked to use the phone, and quickly left. Our friend had a very strange feeling about their questions and general conduct. Two nights later, very late at night, the phone rang. A man asked our friend if he could speak to her husband. When she put her boy friend on the phone, the man at the other end hung up quickly. It is safe to assume that her "helpers" had gotten her phone number when using the phone and were calling back to see if she was alone.

It is not uncommon for someone offering help, once rejected, to ask "You think I'm going to rape you or something?" in a very good-natured tone of voice. Not wanting to seem foolish, we say no, and will let him into our home. There are probably as many times that an offer is genuine as it is potentially dangerous. The problem for us, as women, is that there is no guaranteed way to know which offers of assistance are genuine.

Our recourse in this situation is to limit, as much as possible, the times where we might be in genuine need of help with packages, children, pets, etc. This is not *always* possible. Also, you should know that rapists will offer to help you with packages that obviously are not that heavy. If you do refuse the offer of assistance, it is important to keep on moving, not to stop and talk. If you do accept the offer, stop at your door, thank him, and do not open your door until he is gone. Of course, *never* let anyone know that you live alone. And if he asks if you are afraid he is going to rape you, tell him directly that you do not intend to find out.

Rule Number Nine: We Must Always Act with Graciousness and Openness to Service Personnel

We are trained to be immediately trustful of anyone who allegedly is going to provide our family or home with a service. We feel uncomfortable with being abrupt or asking questions of someone who wants to do us a "favor." In the last few years, more and more women have started asking for proper identification from repair men, delivery men or service personnel. Yet, it often feels as uncomfortable as declining someone's offer of assistance. We also can be caught off guard and forget to ask the appropriate questions.

There was an especially tragic case in this area. A large apartment complex caught on fire. One section was totally destroyed. A week later, a young man went door to door, posing as a smoke detector inspector. Of course he gained entrance to some of the apartments. There was one reported rape as a result.

Women who let men into their homes because of these ploys are not stupid. We have been taught to be co-operative and accommodating when someone is providing a service. And we have been reinforced for that trust level many times with situations that were *not* dangerous. But, again, there is no guaranteed way to discern the ploy from a legitimate offer of service.

We must gamble to figure out who is potentially dangerous and who is not. Any genuine service person should understand your asking for identification and calling the office to confirm it. If it is a male service person, chances are he worries about his family and understands. If the service person is a potential rapist, he will leave immediately and try a more "co-operative" household.

It is our right to cause others minor inconveniences to protect ourselves. There is a myth in this country that we are a community of neighbors and can intrinsically trust all other Americans. This is no longer true. Every community has its stories of someone posing as a police officer or fireman who later turned out to be a criminal. In the spirit of self-caring and the healthy continuation of our own lives, it is imperative that we take precautions to insure our own safety.

The barrier is not so much women not knowing enough to ask for identification and refusing to open doors casually to service personnel. The real barrier is that we feel socially inept or foolish for taking such precautions. These feelings come from not valuing ourselves enough to ask someone else to change their routine in a minor way for our peace of mind. As women, we are asked countless times to rearrange our schedules or interrupt our activities for other people's benefit. We generally do not find that unreasonable, and often will go ahead with changes for another person's sake. We need to ask for some very small changes for *our own sake*. We do not live in an age where we can be totally open to anyone wanting access to our homes. We need to do *whatever* is necessary to insure our own safety. Rape is no longer something that happens in other neighborhoods.

Rule Number Ten: We Must Always Be Compassionate and Helpful with People Less Fortunate than Ourselves

We have closed with what is possibly the strongest rule of etiquette. It is also the dynamic that endangers us the most.

The list of who are less fortunate than us is virtually limitless. Men who are lost or hurt in accidents, acquaintances who have urgent personal problems, people trying to contact our neighbors, etc.—anyone who has fallen onto a moment's misfortune from which only we can rescue them.

This sense of etiquette is perhaps strongest when a woman is approached in her own home. In Seattle, 35 per cent of rape happens in the victim's home. These ruses play on a woman's helping instincts. A man demands that a woman be compassionate, and the more compassionate she is, the better his chances are of forcing his will on her.

In the case of an accident victim, a woman knows that if this man needs medical care she is not trained to give, then letting him in endangers her safety and does him no good. The sooner she calls the police and lets them handle an accident situation, the sooner his needs will be met. But there is great emotional appeal in letting the man enter her home, even if it leaves her vulnerable to rape.

We have been taught to be so trusting that we will let strangers into our homes to use a phone book that could be used as well on the front porch. Or we let a man in rather than direct him to a male neighbor's house or a nearby public place.

Some of the most tragic cases of rape involve a woman responding to a man's request for help. In the Puget Sound area, we had a series of rape murders a few years ago. One of the techniques the assailant used was to approach women with his arm in a cast and ask them to please help him carry or lift something. Two women disappeared from a crowded state park with this man.

Women who respond to this trick are not asking for it; they are following training that has ingrained in them a sense that helping others is an important gesture. A person genuinely needing help in that situation could ask for it of more than one person—a group of men or women—to avoid putting anyone in a potentially dangerous situation. The responsibility for the situation lies *totally* with the offender.

It is not surprising that we as women do not always question the request for help. Again, it is a throwback to a time when we really could interact with strangers, help our neighbors and feel safe. It is also such a major part of our role as mother, wife, nurse and helper that it must seem innate by now. Responding to the many requests we encounter to be helpful or supportive is not a genetically transmitted personality trait. To be helpful or not is a choice we can make at that moment. When we are faced with a request that we think compromises us or one we do not want to honor, there is nothing that dictates that we must react against our own feelings.

Where does this leave us? With the ten rules of etiquette in mind, do we revert to an uncivilized world where we do not speak to strangers and only the strongest survive? Can we expect nothing of other people around us when we need help? Should we create fortresses around our homes to diminish the chances of our being victimized?

We do not need any action that extreme. The first step is to re-examine the general teachings we have discussed and explore how *you* really feel about them. Are you more comfortable paying your own way some of the time? Have you always been a little annoyed at yourself for smiling at people who clearly didn't deserve it? Is your natural inclination to be more firm and inquisitive with people coming to your door, for whatever reasons? For each of our individual personalities, there are unique areas of re-evaluation and change.

There is nothing mysterious about the fact that women in general have not scrutinized "shoulds" and substituted them with dictates that are more healthy and safety enhancing. The women's movement has been instrumental in facilitating this type of consideration. For it to be truly effective, each individual woman must re-examine the expectations for herself. We have evidence that overwhelmingly indicates the need to look twice at these social dictates, and we have the talent and support to make those revisions a reality for all women.

We are not foolish for accepting rules of etiquette. Until now, we have known little else. Also remember that we will all make choices or find ourselves in situations that we might handle differently in the future. If your first response was to let the repair man into your home without any questions, and you find that he intends to do you harm, remember that the potential rape is not your fault. Your opening the door did not make him a rapist. He most likely made that decision before he reached your house. You may want to revise your way of reacting in the future, but that doesn't mean that you provoked or contributed to the crime in any way. You might be a victim in a high-risk situation, but he is still the criminal.

Once we have re-evaluated the roles for ourselves and created our own guidelines, the next step is to examine each situation as it comes up. One of the most seductive aspects of rules of etiquette is that they supply us with easy answers. When we are in a tight spot or have ambivalent feelings about someone's request, our social training is immediately accessible with the answer to our dilemma. The problem is that those answers very often benefit other people and endanger us. With a combination of careful consideration of each situation before making a commitment—or even answering someone's request of us—and the backup of new rules created out of our own sense of what is good for us, we can curtail the almost immediate reflex of overruling our own best interest.

One of the first steps a woman needs to take in her own best interest is the re-evaluation of the rules that dictate our social behavior. If we have some understanding of potentially dangerous situations before we find ourselves in the midst of them, it will be much easier to act in a definitive, effective way. The time to re-evaluate the need to accept "help" from strangers is not after the fact—after he has pushed you into your home when he carried your packages to your front door. The time to re-evaluate is before it happens.

And again, if you do go along with convention in any of these areas, be aware that your decision is *not* irrevocable. You have not been a conspirator in your own rape because you let your date pay for dinner and a movie. Keep your limits in mind, and once he passes those limits, be able to act for yourself.

Also remember that most police will be responsive if you report a bothersome person at your home or a menacing stranger. We can be confused about when to call the police. We may see the same man who approached us go to other houses but hesitate to call because nothing has happened yet. Most police officers would rather investigate and resolve a suspicious-situation call than take a rape report minutes later.

To remedy all of this confusion, we must consider ourselves worthwhile. We must be convinced that we, too, possess basic rights. When a woman values herself, she gets angry when someone assumes she exists for his entertainment or nurturing. When she gets angry, she defends herself.

We sometimes forget our own priorities, the first of which should be the healthy continuation of our own lives—important to us and those who really love us. As women, we must re-examine some of the long-standing traditions in etiquette that delay or prevent our healthy response to a potentially dangerous situation.

III

Self-concept

How well a woman defends herself depends directly on how she feels about herself. If she is more concerned about the rapist's rights and emotional health than her own, she will not defend herself well.

If she doubts her right to make a scene and attract attention, the attack will probably continue. If she ignores her intuition which says a situation is dangerous and instead perceives a man's advances as his brand of flattery, she has a better chance at being raped. If she takes time to ponder the moral and political implications of telling someone to go away, the situation will likely develop beyond the point where she can successfully convince him to go away. Self-doubt and mistrust of our own gut-level feelings are the greatest barriers to quick reflexes.

One characteristic that most women have in common is that we have been taught that valuing ourselves is selfish and undesirable. No matter what our age, social or economic status, sexual or political persuasion, the message is clear that to genuinely like yourself is to be conceited and immodest. It is noble to be restless and discontent with what we have. If we want to work ourselves out of a depression, the answer lies in volunteer work, involvement in other people and generally "getting out of ourselves." Unfortunately, too few of us have ever paid enough attention to ourselves to find out how wonderful we really are.

Low self-esteem, poor self-concept or self-critical behavior are just different ways of expressing the same pain. In general, they all manifest the absence of self-love. Specific to sexual assault, they mean that we may be chosen as victims, that we will put others' rights before ours, that we allow others to intrude into our territory, and most important, that we feel helpless to do anything about it.

There has been some exciting research and treatment recently in the area of poor self-concept in women. There are some specific ways we behave when we don't feel good about ourselves that are relevant to sexual assault. We have chosen only a few examples of the many forms of low self-esteem.

First is the "Black Cloud." If someone says something negative to us, such as, "Your house doesn't look very clean today, have you been sick?" or, "That report was awfully late, what's going on?" we will generalize that negative statement to apply to all aspects of our personality. In a "Black Cloud" state of mind we conclude, "I am really a sloppy person; how do others live with me?" or, "I guess I'm not very reliable; I'm surprised I still have a job." To some degree, this phenomenon is familiar to all of us. A more realistic response for us would be, "Yes, the house does look terrible today, but I usually am good about keeping it clean," or, "Well, I'm glad that I'm usually punctual with my work and this doesn't happen all the time." Even if we are sloppy all of the time or chronically late with our work, it is a faulty generalization to conclude we are not worthwhile people. We need to recognize that we have a problem in that specific area and improve; all is not hopeless, and after all, we are not total zeros as people. A woman with this outlook has a greater chance of improving than the woman who generalizes negative feedback to mean that she is a terrible person who can't be helped.

In the realm of unwanted approaches or sexual assaults, the existence of the "Black Cloud" syndrome is used to the advantage of the offender. Many times in the quasi-social situation, a potential rapist will ask something of a woman. If she even tentatively refuses, he criticizes her. He may say something like, "Well, you're not very friendly, are you? What do you think you are, too good for me or something?" Here we have the double-whammy. First, the criticism that she is not friendly can be translated by the woman into "Black Cloud-isms": "He sees that I'm a cold and harsh person and not very nice to those around me." She might compensate for that by becoming friendly toward him—exactly what he wanted. Second, he accuses her of the all-time criminal offense for women—feeling that she is a good person. A more helpful message for her would be, "No, I'm not friendly toward him. I have a wonderful capacity to be friendly toward people when I want to. As for being better than him, I don't know him well enough to judge yet, but it seems a distinct possibility."

In short, the "Black Cloud" syndrome ups the ante; it increases the scope of what we need to defend. Defending the worth of your entire being to a non-intimate person is not in the scope of what anyone has the right to expect. Accepting that sweeping message and trying to compensate for it is what often leads us to trouble.

The second manifestation of poor self-concept is "Expectations of Perfection." Kate Millet wrote, in *Flying*, that a true indication of maturity was not measuring your accomplishments by their limitations.

These feelings of *only* absolute perfection being justification for rejoicing come to us as small girls. If we were learning a difficult subject in school and got eight out of ten of the test questions right, we were often asked why we missed the two questions. Compliments or encouragement were not given for the eight we got right. In the same vein, potential rapists will criticize you for what you *haven't* done for them.

An example of this is the man who spends a lot of money on a woman during a date. She was probably great company and they had a good time, but the imperfection in the evening is that she will not have sexual intercourse with him. Although she has been a gracious and interesting woman throughout the evening, she is not the *perfect* woman because she is repressing her "natural" desire to sleep with him. How many wives have been sexually overpowered by their husbands who felt the wife was imperfect in her ability to meet his every demand?

The closer we are to someone, the more time we have spent with them, the easier it is to be convinced that we are imperfect, and this one little concession (letting him into your house, giving him your phone number, letting him stay the night) will restore you to perfection. We think the day is coming when we as women are less vulnerable to this type of manipulation. As we know ourselves better and are secure in knowing what attributes we have, we will be less influenced by biased outsiders' appraisals of our worthiness.

The third conspirator in our low self-esteem is our inability to accept compliments. When I first started the Rape Prevention Forum, it was not uncommon for members of the audience to approach me and compliment me on my speaking ability. I would usually dismiss them very quickly, feeling extremely uncomfortable. On the other hand, if any one of those women had come up to me and said, "That's the most ridiculous thing I've ever heard in my entire life," they would have had my attention for hours. Too many of us are more comfortable with negative feedback (without ever questioning its validity) than we are with positive feelings from others.

A potential rapist may be well aware of this. If he can sense that the woman he is approaching is uncomfortable with the compliments he is giving, he may increase the pressure to the point where she feels she must live up to his image of her (which is usually compliant and "nice"), or she might feel she must pay him some compliment in return for being so unusually positive about her. There may be many positive things about this woman. But because she is not encouraged to recognize them in herself, the potential rapist may be the first "overdose" of admiration and value that she has received. It is confusing and can skew the woman's natural inclination to remove herself from the situation. The rapist counts on her not wanting to offend someone who is being so nice.

There are many reasons why we don't accept compliments well. We haven't had much of a chance to practice accepting them; perhaps we just don't believe them or are afraid that if we let the person know us any better, they will find out that all those good things they said weren't really true after all. If we can just accept the compliment at its face value, take it in at that moment, and feel it is the honest opinion of one person, to whom we owe *nothing* for merely expressing his opinion, we will be less vulnerable to this very slick game.

Fourth, "Catastrophic Expectations" contribute to increased vulnerability. Our friend in front of the pizza parlor had catastrophic expectations about what would happen if she told those two men to stop fondling her breasts. She expected a large group of people to ridicule her for her height and generally make her feel humiliated. In reality, what would have probably happened is that the men would have stopped because of the threat of someone on the street intervening. If anyone had stopped to help, the chances of their noticing that the woman in distress was 5'9" is unlikely.

A woman approached by a man wanting to come in and write a message to the next door neighbor may have expectations of the man returning to the neighbor (if she does not let him in) telling the neighbor how rude she was, and the neighbor disliking her. She expects the creation of an unpleasant situation because she won't let him in.

Like other forms of self-criticism, we have been rewarded for feeling that way. If we have catastrophic expectations of the results of our behavior, we can feel helpless. Often in the past when we felt helpless, someone (usually a man) came to our aid. That very act of someone intervening for us convinces us that catastrophe was, in fact, just around the corner. If it wasn't, why would he have helped?

There is no easy way out of this mind set. Experience in trusting your feelings and experiencing *non*-catastrophes as a result is the key. It seems many of us have made progress with problems in different areas of our lives. We should begin to reassure our sisters that we need not always be concerned about those catastrophes. We can tell each other that in our experience not accepting a ride but fixing the tire ourselves did not lead to three days on the side of the highway with no food or water. We can assure each other that going back to work did not cause insanity in our children. We can tell each other going home alone did not result in the dark despair and a lifetime of loneliness we expected. None of this is easy, we *must* remember that. But if we can free our energy and talent from the expectation of catastrophe, we will have more to work with.

The last area of behavior that relates directly to our victimization is "Critical Tapes." Few of us have escaped this, yet we all seem to feel we are the only ones who experience it. It consists of voices that go on inside our heads telling us we are no good. If we trip, a voice immediately says, "You sure are clumsy." That may be blatantly untrue. The only *really* accurate statement you could make about that is "I just tripped over something." We find ourselves using everyday inescapable mistakes or actions to put ourselves down.

Many men are aware of this general dynamic. In the middle of a potentially dangerous situation, a woman's "Critical Tapes" will say something to the effect of, "How did I get myself into this? I should have known he would drive somewhere else. I'm so stupid, I don't know if I'll ever get out of this one alive." This effectively stops us from thinking how we are going to protect ourselves because we are too busy telling ourselves how inept we are.

We often receive cues directly from the potential rapist. If he tells us we can't take care of ourselves and we need him to see us home, a "Critical Tape" will tell us, "Well, maybe he's right. If someone stopped me, I wouldn't know what to do, and I remember that one time I was walking home . . ." The tapes are so subtle, we often do not realize we are buying his message.

The solution to this is fairly straightforward. First, keep track of what your most common tapes are. Counting them is a good way to measure the areas in which you are most self-critical. After you know what some of them are, *replace them with positive statements*. If you can't think of anything right away, have some women friends help you. Sometimes we think: "Here is one of those salesmen at my door again. Oh, I never know what to say. I always end up buying stuff I don't want. I can't get rid of him." Instead, tell yourself, "I'm very direct in other areas of my life and I can learn to be direct in this situation too." With that type of attitude, you will find it *possible* to be direct with the salesman. Before, you were telling yourself that it was beyond the realm of possibility. This is a very important piece of behavior to change—not only for your own safety, but for the enjoyment of yourself as well.

You might be thinking, "But what if it *is* true that I can't ever get rid of these salesmen, then what?" The answer is to do the same thing described above. Find a positive message related to the problem area. *Replace the negative message with a positive message.* That in itself will not resolve the problem, but it will put you in a mind set that makes resolution possible. It probably is true that you never got rid of salesmen *in the past*. That is not the worst fault in the world, and it does not warrant your continually being in danger by letting salesmen into your home.

There is a time and place to examine our faults. If you are faced with an intrusive salesman, that is not the time for you to evaluate your lack of skill in this area. In order to change the behavior, we need to assume that we have the power, insight and talent to make the change. If we are always telling ourselves that we are not too bright, terribly inept, inherently helpless and beyond hope, then our prognosis for change is not too good, is it? Solid recognition of the wealth of good in us is the first important step to changing poor self-concept. After all, we have made it this far under some fairly adverse conditions. That is not the result of any intrinsic worthlessness.

There are a couple of other forms of low self-esteem that do not relate directly to rape prevention, but they do wear and tear on the good self-image we all need. The first is body image. This country is inundated with propaganda about what the normal woman's body should look like. Because 99.9 per cent of us do not have that type of body, we can feel inferior in comparison to the "standard." We also often have incomplete knowledge about the beauty of our body types. Other cultures value the mature woman's body or the rounder body type. Not understanding or liking our bodies is a hard barrier to overcome. It is integral to our feelings of self-worth.

In the same line of thought, we often compare ourselves to other people. This is a no-win situation for three reasons. First, if we compare ourselves to another woman, we probably are going to find her to be "better" than we are. This is demoralizing, often inaccurate and really doesn't accomplish anything. Second, if we do find that we think *we* are better than another person, our tendency is to discount that right away, because we are uncomfortable with the "conceit" of considering ourselves better than someone else. And last, comparison or hero-worship is really a waste of our precious energy. The time and energy we put into idolizing or scrutinizing someone else could be put to much better use by paying attention to ourselves, rewarding ourselves for what is good and striving to change what we want to change. Comparison of self to other people is a very common form of low self-esteem.

How can a woman tell if she has poor self-concept? Generally, it is a feeling that is easily identified. There is an absence of self-love, dominant feelings of helplessness and beliefs that we do not measure up to standard. Remember that it is possible to have low self-esteem in just one or two areas of your life. You may feel very confident in your work and friendships yet feel very inept at intimate relationships. It is also possible, in fact probable, to have the degree or area of low self-esteem change over the course of your life.

Almost all of us feel depressed or dissatisfied because of circumstances from time to time. A poor self-concept is an attitude that carries over to many different situations and through different periods of time. For many reasons, we are trained to have poor self-concepts, so there is nothing alarming about the great numbers of women who feel inadequate and helpless. To get an idea of where you might be on this issue, consider some of the following questions. Add some of your own from your observation of women who don't like themselves very much. Also, examine how each of these characteristics target you as a potential victim:

1. Do you discount yourself when you describe what you do, such as, "I'm *only* a teacher," or, "I'm *just* a housewife"?
2. Do you qualify your statements with, "This is only my opinion," or, "I haven't really thought about this, but . . ."?
3. Do you ask other people's permission to speak ("Can I say something?") or thank others for something you have done?
4. Does your general body language reflect a poor self-concept?
5. Do you have a hard time looking people in the eyes or holding your head up high?
6. Does your voice trail off at the end of a sentence?
7. Do you allow people to interrupt you a lot?
8. Do you slouch, shuffle, fidget or have poor posture when you walk or stand still?
9. Do you find yourself often making comparisons between yourself and others?
10. Are you very quiet in groups of people because you don't feel you have anything worth saying or you don't want to seem stupid?
11. When faced with a new task or the possibility of a different experience, do you assume you will fail before you try?
12. Do you feel you need the help of other people in most things you do?
13. Do you have a hard time accepting compliments?
14. Do you dwell on the negative feedback that you get?
15. Do you tell yourself you are not good at many things?

All of us would answer yes to at least some of these things. That does not mean that we are worthless, that our attitude provokes victimization or that it validates our feeling of poor self-worth. Answering yes to any of those questions means only that we can identify a specific area to work on for increasing self-esteem. In the specific realm of sexual assault, it is important to understand how any one of those behaviors can make us more vulnerable.

It is perfectly natural for women to have self-doubts. There are a variety of theories to explain why this is so. Some people attribute our feelings of low self-esteem to the low value placed on the role of women in this society. Others feel it is due to exclusion from opportunities (available to men) that teach us that we cannot master our own environment. All of us have seen women older than ourselves operate from a stance where they felt inadequate, needed other people's help constantly, and yet seemed to function. This type of role modeling has a large influence. Still others say our language contributes to our poor sense of self. When everything we read is written in the masculine gender, it is more difficult for us to identify with it. The strongest and most documented theory has to do with sex-role stereotyping.

The reasons for our poor self-concept vary among individual women. Whatever reasons are applicable to you, an important aspect of our self-critical behavior is the realization of how it contributes to our victimization. Sex-role stereotyping is a particularly important variable in increasing women's vulnerability to sexual assault.

To demonstrate this point, please imagine that you are a rapist. Rape is a crime of violence, and as a rapist, you are interested in forcing your will on another human being. In order to feel power or control in your own life, you must overcome another person and make that person do something that she doesn't want to do. Pretend you are the rapist and pick five personality characteristics that will be important to you to successfully complete the rape.

1.

2.

3.

4.

5.

Assume that you are ready to look for a victim. What five characteristics are you looking for in her? Keep in mind the setting and time you have chosen.

1.

2.

3.

4.

5.

The chart on page 37 contains twenty-seven attributes considered healthy in adult males and eleven in adult females. The chart was taken (and revised) from the Broverman[14] study of seventy-nine mental-health professionals. In the study, the clinicians were asked what constituted a healthy male, a healthy female and a healthy adult. What the researchers discovered was that the healthy male and healthy *adult* descriptions were almost the same. The description of the healthy female was very different. An additional point is the fact that men are the proto-type to which we are compared and against which we are judged.

Did you find many of your five rapist's characteristics in the column for healthy male? Did you find many of the victim's characteristics in the healthy fe-male column? The point of this exercise is to demonstrate the influence of sex-role stereotyping (and the value we place on those characteristics) in the male dom-inant/female submissive dynamic of rape.

Return again to your imagination. Imagine you are the rapist about ready to make an approach. What would happen if you walked up to a man and said, "Don't scream and you won't get hurt"? How do you think he would respond? What if you approached a woman and said, "Don't scream and you won't get hurt"? Can you imagine the distinct differences in the possible responses? Thus, the bottom line is that if you want to be violent in America, and be successful in your approach and execution of the crime, your chances of success are greatest if you choose women as your victims. Not because we are biologically inferior or because we provoke the crime. Simply because we embrace the attributes we have been taught to embrace. Those are attributes that limit our potential, leave us feeling helpless and make us vulnerable to crimes and an unhappy state of mind.

MALE-VALUED AND FEMALE-VALUED STEREOTYPIC ITEMS

HEALTHY MALE ATTRIBUTES

Very aggressive
Very independent
Not at all emotional
Almost always hides emotions
Very objective
Not at all easily influenced
Very dominant
Likes math and science very much
Not at all excitable in a minor crisis
Very active
Very competitive
Very logical
Very worldly
Very skilled in business
Very direct
Knows the way of the world
Feelings not easily hurt
Very adventurous
Can make decisions easily
Never cries
Almost always acts as a leader
Very self-confident
Not at all uncomfortable about being
  aggressive
Very ambitious
Easily able to separate feelings from
  ideas
Not at all dependent
Never conceited about appearance

HEALTHY FEMALE ATTRIBUTES

Very talkative
Very tactful
Very gentle
Very aware of feelings of others
Very religious
Very interested in own appearance
Very neat in habits
Very quiet
Very strong need for security
Enjoys art and literature very much
Easily expresses tender feelings

The attributes in the "healthy female" column of the chart are not all negative. We enthusiastically agree that many of those traits should be present in all human beings. We would not necessarily want some of the attributes in the "healthy male" column. We need to move toward a more even distribution of those traits. If each individual could develop whatever characteristics suited her/him best, we would have healthy adult attributes relevant to both healthy men and healthy women. We could amplify the differences between the sexes without the healthy adult male equaling healthy adult and the healthy female equaling victim.

Another important discovery relevant to our victimization was provided by Martin Seligman.[15] His theory is known as "learned helplessness." In a series of experiments, Dr. Seligman put dogs in a box with two compartments. The dogs would be shocked while in one compartment, but they quickly learned that they could jump to the other compartment and escape the shock. Another set of dogs were put into a harness in the box and shocked repeatedly. They were not allowed to jump to the other compartment. After a short while, they learned that nothing they did made a difference in the intensity and frequency of the shocks. Later they were released from the harness. Still believing that they were helpless, they never learned to jump into the other compartment. They simply sat there and endured the shock, as if they were still in the harness.

It might seem farfetched to compare women to the harnessed dogs in this experiment. The comparison certainly isn't flattering. But the essence of the results is that after a period of time of believing that there was nothing they could do, the dogs reacted helplessly. Our parallel training that tells us we are physically inept, socially provocative and the rapist is not to be deterred causes a similar result.

In some actual rape cases, there is literally nothing a woman can do about the incident. Not having any choice does not make her stupid, silly, immature or inept. But the effect of this type of "learned helplessness" is to reinforce our generally poor sense of self, and specifically, our sense of not being able to control the situation when approached in a quasi-social situation. "Learned helplessness" is yet another logical and natural extension of healthy female attributes not relating at all to healthy adult attributes. "Learned helplessness" is an expected result from a society where women are discouraged from mastering their environment.

In one sense, our learning a helpless stance is an enormous paradox. As girls, we were punished differently than boys. Our punishment often included withdrawal of love, had an interminable time span and only ended after we apologized. Many of us remember apologizing for incidents when we were not sure what we had done wrong. Worse yet, we would apologize when we *knew* we had done nothing wrong. We were taught that if we said we were sorry, we could find ourselves in the person's good graces once again. Thus, we learned that we have the power to fix things we don't understand simply by saying, "I'm sorry."

In the realm of sexual assault, we can see this paradox at its most confusing level. Going on our past theory that the apology will get us out of an uncomfortable situation or soothe our date's ego, we will often offer our apologies for giving him the wrong impression, or letting him spend all that money. Of course, the issue really isn't the money or what type of woman you are. Therefore, the apology doesn't touch the real issue—the attacker's need to force his will on you. Our one great source of power—our apology—renders us helpless if that is all we have to rely on. This paradox also leads us to believe that our control comes from discounting what we feel or know. No *real* power can have a person's disbelief in herself as its base.

Those of us who feel emotionally inadequate to deal with sexual assault also feel physically inadequate. Given the average woman's background, we do not readily have the experience and skills we need when we reach adulthood.

We become convinced in early life that there is no way we can hurt men. When we wrestle with our brothers and can't get out of the holds, we learn that we are ineffective fighters. Perhaps we can scratch, but that, we are warned, makes men want to hurt us. It never occurs to men that their physical aggression against us might make us want to hurt them.

As two bodies come together forcefully, both people are experiencing the pain of bodily contact. The difference between a rapist and a victim is that the rapist probably has more experience with bodily contact, while the victim may be encountering forceful contact for the first time. The rapist may have a long history of tackle football, soccer, neighborhood and barroom fights, or military training.

The most bodily contact the victim may have ever received is a spanking. Little girls are usually channeled into more sedate leisure activities that do not reveal the human body's tolerance for pain and injury. Young girls may never learn what it is like to overcome an opponent. It is this kind of experience that gives the rapist the advantage and renders the victims inadequate.

There is another element in team sports participation that aids the rapist. Winning can give boys feelings of confidence and familiarize them with their bodies and physical talents. Girls do not participate in contests of the same intensity. Contests they do participate in (volleyball, touch football, folk dancing, etc.) are less socially admirable than boys' games. The result can be that girls gain less confidence and never know the full potential of their bodies. The first time they must utilize all of their physical reserves might be when they are about to be raped. However, women are now learning that they can fight well and are finally realizing the potential of their own bodies.

Some women are allowed, in childhood, to develop skills that will enhance their safety. These women are called "Tomboys." Tomboyism is considered "cute" and is tolerated for a while before the young woman must enter the dating arena. Girls trying to act like boys are tolerated, whereas boys trying to act like girls are not. Parents rarely introduce their children as, "This is my daughter Mary. She's a Tomboy. And this is my son Jack. He's a Susiegirl." While this paradox is restrictive and oppressive to men, the ultimate insult is aimed at woman. It tells us that the male experience is good and adequate and we allow girls to imitate that, whereas the female experience is degrading and inadequate and we will not let boys imitate that.

If we were "Tomboys" in our childhood, this does not mean that those skills are readily accessible to us as adult women. Studies have documented that women lose the spirit, motivation and agility they had as children. This process usually takes place during adolescence when girls are taught to value more sedate activities. As a child, I rode thoroughbred horses. I was not afraid to jump over fences or to canter very fast. Today, just sitting in the saddle terrifies me. I had no traumatic experience with horses. I stopped riding at age eleven when we moved to another city. From then on, I was a "normal" teen-age girl, more interested in boys, cosmetics and short-story writing.

Nowhere is the expected superiority of male behavior over female behavior more apparent than in the early confrontations we all encounter. If a son is bullied by another boy, his father might teach him how to fight and insist that he fight back and defend himself. If a child bullied a girl, one or both of the parents may contact the child and/or the child's parents to defend their daughter's honor. They may even tell the daughter to ignore the bullying. Few parents realize that later in life their daughter might be bullied by a rapist, and she will not have her parents on hand to defend her, nor can she ignore him.

In essence, our previous experience with physical aspects of our lives detracts from our own defense. Compared with the experience of some rapists, our lack contributes to our vulnerability.

Yet women have borne children, worked in deplorable conditions and taken major responsibility for family life and business. This is not the behavior of an inherently submissive sex. For centuries we have done without safe and adequate birth control, complete and accurate sex education, equal rights in the legal and economic system, and reliable health care. But we are told to be quiet and make the best of it.

The conclusion we can draw is that women feel little control over their own lives. Perhaps men feel little control over their lives too, but helpless feelings have an enormous impact on a woman faced with an assault situation. If she feels little control over the direction of her life, choice of employment, control of pregnancy and where she will live and travel, then it is hard to believe that this same woman will be composed, quick to act and successful in taking control of an assault situation.

In addition, women are generally defined by their relationships with men and how others perceive those relationships. A man can be without a primary relationship and still maintain a healthy self-concept if he is successful in his job or has numerous relationships with women. The woman without a partner is suspect.

Women are not supposed to derive the same fulfillment from autonomy that men do. We learn not to make and act on independent decisions. We learn others may be able to do things better. Thus, rapists can almost always give instructions to their victims, confident that women will follow their orders. They less frequently expect another man to follow those instructions.

One of the most damaging consequences of our own poor self-concept is that we treat other women as its source. We cannot say that men make better companions, are more interesting and trustworthy, and say that women are catty, jealous and inferior without meaning that about ourselves as well. We cannot make such statements about all women and mean all women except ourselves.

Women need each other as resources. We need each other to help rebuild healthy self-concepts. We need to go places with each other to reduce the chance of being assaulted, rather than always relying on men to escort us for protection. We can protect ourselves. Most of all, women need to learn from each other and care for each other. It is only from sharing with someone from a common background that we can understand our own roots and continue to live with the self-love, dignity and confidence we deserve.

So, now we know we might have a poor self-concept. Most of us didn't need this book to tell us that. We could stand to feel better about ourselves. We have some clues as to where these feelings come from, and we know how they manifest themselves in the realm of sexual assault. What next?

It would be irresponsible to pretend to fully address such an important concern with just a few suggestions. There are many self-concept groups (self-help with other women) around the country. Good assertiveness training will take any woman a long way toward realizing her own value.

In the interim, we think you will find the exercises in the next section helpful and strongly encourage you to participate in those exercises. We also encourage you to talk with other women about these same issues. You can give each other good feedback and reduce your sense of isolation. There is nothing like a partner in this process to remind you of the progress you are making. If there is a self-help group in your area—through the YWCA, mental-health center, a religious order or perhaps a local Rape Relief Clinic—it would expedite matters to belong to it.

The "What-if Games" in the next section are very important. Work on changing the outcome of situations you anticipate from negative to positive, just as you are trying to convert the messages in your head. Create a hierarchy of situations you find difficult—where you feel you will never master the task. Start with what is potentially the least difficult task and then go at it. To this day, I can remember the thrill I had when I finally attempted to pump my own gas at a self-service station. After a lifetime of mystery surrounding that task and belief that it was dirty and beyond my mechanical ability, I experienced a sense of power at finally conquering the gas pump. All of us have tasks for which we have "learned helplessness." Start with the smallest and work on up. Be sure the tasks are gradually more difficult.

And remember that this process is often discouraging and sometimes painful. This is where other women, with healthy attributes, can help you. The long-run pay-off will be feelings of control over your own life, confidence in yourself and a more realistic sense of self-esteem. We all have good reason to care about ourselves. It is about time we start!

We would like to end this chapter with the quote that we use at the end of each Rape Prevention Workshop. It validates our right to a good self-concept. "Don't compromise yourself, you're all you've got."

IV

Seven Exercises

EXERCISE I

First Thoughts

How good you feel about yourself will directly dictate how well you defend yourself. If you don't like yourself very well, you will have a hard time defending yourself. When you are approached, if the first thoughts in your mind are: I don't want to make a scene; maybe he's not going to hurt me, he's just trying to flatter me in his own strange way; or simply, I don't want to hurt his feelings, then you will not be reacting quickly enough to get yourself to safety.

Your first thoughts should be of your own value and safety. It should immediately occur to you that no one has the right to physically or emotionally hassle you. The bottom line is that you are convinced that you deserve to be around tomorrow in the same shape that you are today. But that is easier said than done.

We are all very aware of what we don't like about ourselves. To say anything complimentary about ourselves is being conceited and immodest. We cannot stress enough the importance of caring about yourself and reacting quickly as a result. Without a positive self-concept, the pizza parlor incident that happened to our friend is commonplace.

Certainly all of us can find some good reasons for caring about ourselves, but we don't get to talk about them very much. As a result, sometimes the negative feelings we do express dominate. That's not helpful in an assault situation. To get into this positive frame of mind, which we all deserve, it is best to look closely at the *specific* aspects we *like* about ourselves.

Think of three reasons why *you* should be around tomorrow. Write those down on three index cards and put them around the house where you will see them often. Repeat the sentence, "I think I should be around here tomorrow because . . ." whenever you come across a card.

Now look over this list of reasons women in our workshop gave for wanting to be here tomorrow:

There is still too much in life I'd like to experience.

I know that I am able to take care of myself—to be independent—so I'd like to do it for the rest of my life.

I have just now started to discover myself and my abilities. I want to live to see what life's like. I want to live and be here tomorrow because

I love to see my family work and have fun and just because I don't want to die.

I believe that I have an artistic talent that I want to share with others. Also, I want to experience a lot of living in my life yet.

I like living and discovering myself.

I enjoy watching my creativity unfold.

I am meeting a lot of stimulating people now and deserve to be able to expand those relationships, and no one has the right to take that away.

I should be around tomorrow because I love the earth, know how to take care of it and can continue to make it a better place to live.

I am a neat person. I have a lot to offer people. I am a good listener.

I like myself and other people and I feel I have a lot to give.

I love life and every day I try to learn new things. It makes me a more rounded person. I can help others and vice versa.

I am honest and open and will talk about anything to people, which works as a catharsis and validation.

I am accepting of people and what they have to offer without passing judgment.

I should be around tomorrow because I deserve to do the things I have planned for my life.

I like the fact that I have the capacity to be very creative. I like the fact that I am able to learn things easily. I like the fact that I'm able to make decisions and live with them.

I've really learned to care for myself before others' needs and to set my goals. I am only concerned with my well-being.

I am not intimidated by other people.

I'm sensitive to other people's feelings, but I also won't be hassled.

I am persistent when times are tough and optimistic even when goals are far off.

I am becoming more assertive. I am placing more value in my relationships with women, rather than men. I am using and developing my creativity. I am striving for greater independence.

I have the ability to develop friendships that are more than superficial. I like to make others laugh.

I can see the other person's viewpoint before deciding mine.

I have determination, achievement, and control over my life.

I think I am a good listener to whom people can talk. I like to think I have a good sense of humor.

I like my ability to see the best of a situation or event and the "plus" aspects of other people; I'm an unflappable optimist.

I like my honesty, assertiveness, sense of humor, and intelligence.

The thing I like best about myself is my honesty and fairness. Honesty in any situation is very important to me.

I enjoy my problem-solving and investigative interests and ability.

I am understanding, and I fight for my rights. I like to do things and meet people.

I appreciate my sense of humor; it gets me through a lot.

I like knowing that I'm willing to stand up for my rights—I am not easily verbally intimidated.

I have an inner drive and the necessary determination to improve my life. I know what I want and I am pursuing it.

I am creative with ideas and in forming relationships between things and words. I am also artistic in various crafts.

I have the ability to get along with any kind of person.

I like being organized at work and at home. I like knowing that I can find things when I want them. I like being neat at work. I'm a secretary.

Surely some of these statements must apply to you as well, even if you haven't thought of them. Write down those that fit you on an index card. Add those positive aspects which you haven't listed yet. Make a thick stack of index cards. Carry them with you. When you have a free moment, on a bus, at home, at work or school, take out the top card. Repeat what it says and really think about it for a while, then put it on the bottom of the deck.

This exercise is greatly enhanced when it is done with other people. If you live with a roommate or group of people, we suggest that you incorporate this exercise into your daily routine. Each person in an office or class or family makes a positive statement about him or herself and follows it with a positive statement about another person in the group. We have done this in our workshops, and it has two excellent advantages.

First, it gives you extra ideas for your deck of positive cards. Second, you find out that someone noticed some aspect of you that you never knew they were aware of. We feel strongly that this is a good exercise for mothers and daughters.

Many of us can think of negative aspects of our personality. That is not at all relevant to this exercise. The focus here is to recognize and attend to the *good* aspects as much as we usually dwell on the less-than-good.

Once you are fully comfortable with the belief that you are worth defending, then perhaps you might want to pay attention to some of your negative aspects and change them. In that process, you can add another positive to your deck of cards—that you are strong and mature enough to recognize your faults and change them.

EXERCISE II

Body Language

It is an old myth that if you carry yourself in a provocative manner, you are asking to be raped. However, how you carry yourself is an indication to a potential rapist about how you feel about yourself and generally how submissive you are.

If you walk along as if you are sorry for the space you take up, it will be the rapist's guess that you will submit if he threatens you. It will take most of us a lot of practice before we walk as though we know where we are going, and no one is going to stop us.

Begin with a very round-shouldered, slouched body position that looks as if you are embarrassed. Really get the feel of it. Think in terms of the placement of your head and neck, shoulders, arms, trunk and foot position. Then work on each area separately, straightening them out. When you feel your head is erect, your shoulders back, your arms at your sides, your trunk thrust forward and your feet pointing straight ahead, exaggerate your stance. Put this stance in motion by marching in an exaggerated manner.

As a good point of reference, you might want to have a photograph taken of your present body stance. After three months of conscious effort to change your body language, have another photograph taken and compare the difference.

EXERCISE III

Eye Contact

Eye contact is one of the most important components of the assertive attitude. No matter how assertively you speak, if you are not looking the person in the eye, it won't be convincing.

If you have a hard time maintaining eye contact, start with an inanimate object, maybe a chair. Stare at the lower right leg of the chair. Next stare at the lower left leg, at the left arm, at the right arm, the back of the chair and, finally, the head rest. Repeat the exercise until you become familiar with the sensation of fixing your eyes on something for extended periods of time.

If you are uncomfortable staring at an inanimate object, practice eye contact with the newscasters on the television. It would be best if you started with the sound turned down. Repeat this exercise until you look the newscaster in the eye without thinking about it.

Often, looking someone *directly* in the eye is hard for us. Remember that concentrating your focus at another point around the eye (eyebrows, tear ducts, nose, etc.) has the same effect on the person you are looking at. This is an excellent solution for those of us who are intimidated by direct eye contact.

Eventually, practice with a sympathetic partner. Following the same routine as you did with the chair, stare at your partner's right foot, left foot, knees, hips, waist, right elbow, left elbow, shoulders, neck, chin, mouth and, finally, eyes. You may want someone to call out instructions at timed intervals. Have that person give you her reaction to the steadiness of your eye contact.

EXERCISE IV

Tone of Voice

Here we repeat the principles used to achieve good body posture. Start with a helpless, inaudible voice. Use the same phrases over and over again; phrases like, "I don't want to talk to you." "Will you leave me alone!" "I will start yelling if you don't leave."

Gradually lower the pitch of your voice and increase its volume. Practice at each stage for a while. The ultimate will be when your natural voice is yelling and increasing your adrenalin. If you do this in the mirror, you will see the change in facial expression. Practice with a partner who can tell you how you sound.

EXERCISE V

Assertive Sentence Structure

We have constant opportunities to practice assertive sentence structure. Daily we are confronted by salespersons whose products we don't want, political or religious representatives who want to talk with us, and common panhandlers. If you can't say "no" to any of these people, you can't say "no" to a rapist.

To start with, follow this order of practice situations—unwanted telephone calls, in-person salespeople, on-the-street political or religious representatives and panhandlers. Your difficulty in saying "no" may fall on a different continuum. If so, reorganize the list to fit you.

Since your goal is to act assertively in getting rid of these people, you need phrases or words that come quickly to mind and are effective. While you are going about your daily business, repeat different phrases to yourself, not concentrating on tone of voice, but simply on becoming familiar enough with them that they are automatic. Here are some suggestions:

Thank you, but I have all the (life insurance, cosmetics, funeral plots) that I need.

No, I don't want any literature today.

Please let me pass by.

No, I do not have any money for you.

If we act non-assertively, these people take our time and energy and we end up being angry with ourselves, which takes more time and energy. We gain more peace of mind by stating exactly what we want and don't want. Also, the other person isn't wasting time and energy that could be used to approach someone who really is interested.

Following are some general thoughts you need to consider:

1. Remember that your first priority is your own continued good health. Trust your intuition about danger. All of us are responsible for ourselves. It is not necessary for you to endanger your safety to solve a man's problem.

2. Be sure that the word NO is actually in the sentence, preferably at the beginning.

3. Shake your head "no" while you say it. Many of us will say, "I don't know," or "I really don't think I want to do that" while we smile and nod our heads.

4. Be as brief as possible, giving few details. Try to develop short sentences that offer no explanation but can readily come to mind.

5. Boycott the words "I'm sorry." They should not be used at any time by you in the conversation. As an experiment, you might want to count how many times you say "I'm sorry" in a day. It creeps into our conversation much too often.

6. Do not confuse assertiveness with aggression. Telling a person that you do not want to talk with him or that you do not like him is being assertive. Attacking a man's sexual prowess, moral character, mother or wife is being hostile, and as valid as those observations may be, they will provoke anger.

7. Constantly review the eye contact, body language and tone of voice suggestions. How you say it is equally as important as what you say.

In terms of sexual assault, if you rehearse a phrase such as, "Who do you think you are?" an assailant is not likely to answer, "I'm a rapist and I'm on your case tonight." If you yell, "What in the hell do you think you're doing?" he probably will not answer, "I was just going to grab you and pull you into my car." Make a statement; do not ask a question. Say, "Get your hands off me" or "Go away."

In developing any response, try to make it definite. You do not want phrases that require further explanation or invite a conversation. Whatever you say, expect to be asked, "Why not?" or "What's wrong with you?" This goes for assailants as well as salespeople. The best remedy is to firmly repeat what you said the first time. If they didn't get your message then, they were not listening. This broken-record technique is very useful.

Be sure you have decided in advance how many times you are willing to repeat yourself. If you reach your limit and the person is still asking "What's wrong?" or requesting more information, then shut the door, walk down the street or move to another table.

Often the assailant will try to engage you in conversation to wear down your resistance. The broken-record technique is effective in letting him know you know your own mind and will be assertive about it, yet it is important to have a sense of when enough is enough.

Practice your phrases until they come out of your mouth spontaneously. Make sure they replace "I'm sorry," and "Please do not hurt me."

EXERCISE VI

What-if Games

Now that you are convinced that you are worth defending, have direct eye contact, assertive body language, firm tone of voice and concise sentence structure, you are ready to demonstrate your skill.

The purpose of this book is to change your reflex of fear into a reflex of action. It is important to practice your skills and to plan a response whenever possible. This type of preparedness (which the rapist counts on your *not* having) is our most needed defense.

The following are some situations you can plan a response for. Work out a strategy now. After you have read the self-defense portion of the book, return and plan physical follow-up strategies for the same situations.

What if someone asks you to give a message to a neighbor who is out?

What if someone at a beach asks you to help get his canoe out of the water?

What if someone you met at a party and danced with insists on getting your phone number because he thinks the two of you "have a thing"?

What if you are on a date with a man you like? You go to his apartment and as soon as you enter the living room, he tries to force himself on you.

What if you are walking your dog in the park and three teen-agers hassle you?

What if you are carrying two heavy bags of groceries and a strange man asks if he can help you?

What if a man follows you into a public rest room and blocks your exit?

What if you are home alone and a man pounds on your door begging you to let him in because he's been hurt?

It is important to add your own situations to this small list. Remember, too, that there are circumstances, different for each of us, where we would choose submission as our option. Have those situations clearly in mind. And remember that if you are a victim, you are not less of a person.

With this composite of resourceful attitude and awareness, you can now make the most of the physical self-defense techniques. This is a state of mind you deserve!

EXERCISE VII

Timidity, Hostility and Assertiveness

When we began this book, we stated that rape is one of many crimes along a continuum. The available responses we have also fall along a continuum. It is important to understand differences between and results of the various responses.

Most of us find ourselves responding to an unwanted approach in a timid manner at certain times in our lives. The timid (non-assertive) response is characterized by an uncertainty in one's voice, body language, eye contact and content of what one says.

When we are timid, it is most often because we aren't trusting our own feelings and are more concerned about the other person than we are about ourselves. This is readily apparent to the person hassling us, and he pushes until we finally give in to reconcile our own lack of trust in ourselves. In short, the timid response is other-oriented and benefits the person hassling us. It is not a response that protects us. Unfortunately, it is the response we all have been taught and have been rewarded for giving.

At other times in our lives, we are responding in a hostile or aggressive manner. The hostile response changes roles between assailant and victim. When the unwanted approach begins, the man sees himself as the assailant and sees us as the victim. When we respond in a hostile manner, he sees us as the assailant and himself as the victim. From that, he sometimes chooses to "defend himself" by escalating the situation. The hostile response does not address itself to whatever approach he is using. It does not defuse the situation and insure our safety.

A crucial component of the hostile response is physical proximity. In any kind of confrontation, we should be very careful about moving *toward* the assailant. This can immediately trigger in him a feeling of being trapped and needing to fight his way out. If at all possible, we should try to hold our own ground. If you have an unwanted person in your home and you can get to the door, the best idea is probably to keep on going and go to a neighbor's for help. What if your children are there, or some other valuable person or thing is in your home and you are not willing to leave it? If you order the person out of your house, be sure you do not stand by the door or other exit. Open the door, then move away from it. If you stand with the door open next to you, he will wonder what you are going to do to him as he goes out the door. Hostile responses are valuable to us in their liberating effect, but we also need to consider the result.

The third response on the continuum, the one in the middle and the one this book strives for, is the assertive response. In this response, our physical stance conveys the convictions of our words. We answer the approach with a direct statement about our feelings. We trust what we feel and know that we do not owe any explanations to anyone. We are clear about how much we are willing to put up with. We defend our territory both physically and verbally and can easily let the other person know what those limits are. Our tone of voice is calm because we are sure of ourselves. We are able to follow through on whatever we say we will do next.

It is helpful to realize the differences between the available responses. The following chart will be a start. We suggest that you take the unwanted approaches that you encounter most often and draft the three possible responses. It is helpful to clearly see the non-assertive response so we don't slip back into it. That is very easy to do. Working on the hostile responses is good for venting our very legitimate anger. And finally, the assertive response is important to have in mind until it comes naturally for us.

ASSERTIVE SENTENCE STRUCTURE

Possible Responses

HASSLE OR APPROACH UNWANTED	NON-ASSERTIVE TIMID, UNCERTAIN, INSECURE	HOSTILE THREATENING, AGGRESSIVE, HEATED	ASSERTIVE CONFIDENT, SELF-RELIANT, CALM
What's wrong with you? Don't you like me?	Oh, no, I don't want you to think that.	Why should I?	No, I don't.
I thought we had something going. Look at all the money I spent on you.	I'm sorry you spent all that money.	What do you think I am, rental property?	I don't feel we have anything going.
All I want to do is leave a message for the guy next door. It's real important.	Well, I guess that would be all right.	Buzz off! You are really bothering me, stupid!	Go to the manager's office (or a nearby store), write your message, and leave it on his door.
Let me give you a ride home. I don't want anything to happen to you.	Well, I guess maybe I'd better not walk alone.	I can get home by myself, jerk.	No, I am going to walk.
I just need a few minutes of your time to show you this product.	O.K., if it will only take a minute.	Who do you think you are, wasting my time?	I don't need the product.
As long as Jim isn't home right now, why don't you let me in so I can wait and we can talk?	It will be a long time before Jim gets back. I'm not sure what to do.	Why would I want to know you?	I will have Jim call you when he returns. Or: I will let him know you were here. Good-by.

This chart is not a script. It demonstrates the differences in the various responses available to us. Each of us must formulate our own responses.

PART II

Introduction

You've been to a dance. You're waiting for your friends to bring the car from the parking lot when a man you danced with a couple of times drives up and offers you a ride. You turn him down, firmly but politely. He persists in asking you to come with him; you continue to tell him no. Suddenly, undeterred by your firm negative response, he jumps out of the car, grabs you, and shoves you into the car.

You're washing dishes when a man appears in the kitchen doorway and orders you to go into the bedroom and take your clothes off.

It's early morning, cool and pleasant, and you're out running. A man you've often noticed running at the same time catches up with you, nods, wheezes hello, and runs on past. As you pass a bend in the path, he jumps on you from behind some bushes and drags you into them.

It's night and your car has broken down. You're walking to the pay phone a block away when a man runs out of the darkness, grabs you, and yanks you into an alley.

What can you do?

The first part of this book has dealt with verbal self-defense. We've talked about rape myths; about how movies, television and our culture in general condition us to believe those myths. More importantly, we've dealt with learning to be assertive, with improving self-concept, with showing you ways to overcome some of the conditioning that makes us good victims. The first chapters are meant to teach you how to say no so he knows you mean it and is convinced. He may not like you very much for saying no, but that's his problem, not yours.

But what happens when he *isn't* convinced, or when you have no chance to use your assertive skills? In three of the situations described above, the attack came as a total surprise. In the third scene, even though the woman had seen the man several times before, she had no warning of his attack. In the second and fourth scenes, not only was the attack a surprise, the man was a stranger.

Even in the first scene, where the woman and her attacker had had some social contact, he wasn't stopped by her assertiveness. Although a firm negative response—"No, I don't want a ride"; "No, I can carry the bags myself"—can and often does stop a rape attempt, it may not always be enough. No matter how good your eye contact and how firm your voice, telling him "No, I don't want you to do that" when he's knocked you down and is ripping your clothes off probably isn't going to stop him.

So what do you do when you've either had no chance to use your verbal skills or when verbal skills haven't been enough? That's what the second half of this book is about: how to defend yourself physically; how to strike and kick to the body's most vulnerable targets; how to create so much pain in your attacker that he is no longer thinking about rape but only of his pain, thus giving you the opportunity to escape to safety.

GOALS OF SELF-DEFENSE

The primary self-defense goal is quite simple: to create pain in the man who has attacked. However, this goal can be difficult to deal with. No one wants to deliberately hurt another human being. A woman, particularly, is brought up with the idea that to be a "good" woman she must be kind, nurturing, compassionate, gentle, caring. Those are values that should be encouraged in men as well, but they are regarded as being particularly appropriate to women. And, indeed, without those qualities, the world would not be fit to live in. But we must realize that in the context of a violent assault, those qualities must be temporarily put aside. The rapist is not kind, is not gentle, most certainly doesn't give a damn about you and is probably quite willing to hurt you. A gentle response on your part is simply not appropriate. Your appropriate response is rage. There is nothing in this world, *nothing*, that gives this man the right to attack you. When you've been attacked, you have no responsibility for his welfare, only for your own.

So you must strike and kick to hurt. You are far more important than the gratification of a rapist's need to be powerful.

CHOICE

Self-defense is an option; it is something we *can* do, not something we *have* to do. The impression has sometimes been given in the last few years not only that "any woman can" defend herself, but that every woman had *better* do so, and if she doesn't, then there's something the matter with her. As if to say if you don't fight off your attacker, you're (1) stupid, (2) weak and cowardly, (3) clumsy, (4) counter-revolutionary, (5) all of the above.

There are many good reasons why you might choose not to defend yourself in an assault situation, including your religious convictions, your pacifist political feelings, or that you truly feel it would be wrong for you to hurt another person. Therefore, physical self-defense is not something you would do. That is a proper and legitimate choice for you to make.

Another possibility is that after reading this book and thinking about the techniques described here, you conclude that you would not be able to use them successfully. That is, for you, a legitimate choice. It doesn't mean that you're clumsy or stupid or any such thing. It means that you've given the matter some thought, and made the decision you feel is best for you.

On the other hand, suppose you decide you will defend yourself if you are assaulted. But when it happens, it's not a man grabbing you by the arms, it's a man pointing a gun at you. Or instead of one man, it's six or seven. In either case, the best and wisest thing may well be for you not to fight back.

The important thing to remember is that it's a matter of choice and circumstances, and choosing not to fight back is a legitimate choice. Just as I am unhappy with men telling women that they should submit to assault, I am unhappy with women telling other women they have to fight back. Either way, your freedom of choice is being taken away from you.

However, in order to choose, you must have information on which to base your choice. We've all heard that "women should never try to resist; they'll only get hurt worse if they try." What this statement is really saying is that women *can't* defend themselves, which in most cases is simply not true. What is true is that women often *don't know how*.

Most women have no training whatsoever in self-defense—most of us don't even have much experience with contact sports or plain roughhousing. Johnny and David and the other boys on the block grew up rassling and fighting, sometimes in fun, sometimes not. For us, of course, this wasn't "ladylike" activity, and so we probably didn't do it, at least not past puberty. The boys, of course, kept right on.

Nor were we taught where and how to kick or hit when we were the objects of an attempted rape. So our knowledge of how to defend ourselves has been, at best, severely limited.

SUCESSFUL SELF-DEFENSE

Successful self-defense is a skill that can be learned by anyone. There is nothing mysterious or esoteric about it. You don't have to study karate for ten years—or even one year—to be able to defend yourself, though studying a martial art would certainly increase and sharpen your skills. Self-defense is basically simple common sense combined with a little knowledge about how to kick and hit, and what the body's most vulnerable targets are. *Self-defense is not karate, judo or kung fu; it's just plain mean common sense.*

Successful self-defense is made up of three basic components:

1. An absolutely committed response to attack
2. A combination of effective target and technique
3. Trusting your radar

The first is the most important. Once you make that initial choice to defend yourself, and you're in a situation where it's possible, whatever the technique is that you use, DO IT! You cannot be wishy-washy about your response; if you are, it's better to make no response at all. What the technique is may not matter much —you may be able to choose among three or four—but you *must* do it with complete commitment. Suppose you're caught in an emergency and have to hitchhike. Instead of taking you where you need to go, he pulls off to the side of the road and starts moving in on you. One possible response is to poke your elbow into his nose/mouth.

But suppose that instead of using all your strength and power and really smashing him in the face, you sort of pull back at the last second and only hurt him a little bit. What do you think he'll do if he's not incapacitated, he's only hurt a little; instead of being blind with pain, his eyes are just watering a little? His reaction is likely to be what mine is when I'm fixing a broken lamp and get a mild shock: I want to kick the lamp across the room.

Remember: You must hurt him badly enough to *stop* him, not hurt him just enough to make him angry. You must use *all* your speed, *all* your power, and *all* your anger.

The second key to successful self-defense is the combination of an effective technique and a vulnerable target area. There are some things you can do that simply aren't worth the effort, because you're using your body in an inefficient way against a part of his body that is not vulnerable.

Again, let's set up a scene: he's grabbed you around the neck from the front. (1) You yank at his wrists, trying to pull his hands away from your throat. (2) You step forward slightly and smash him in the nose with the heel of your palm.

Do you have much question which will do the job?

The problem with the first situation is that the woman is trying to match her strength against his. This will almost always be a no-win situation for the woman. Most men are somewhat bigger and somewhat stronger than most women. Although crime statistics show that the average rapist is only about three inches taller and twenty pounds heavier than his victim, the fact remains that he's still probably stronger.

Self-defense is not a contest of strength. Your ability to defend yourself does not depend in any way on your ability to bench press 300 pounds. We're too used to thinking in terms of muscular strength—or lack thereof—and need to think instead in terms of vulnerability. Suppose your attacker weighs 212 pounds and is a weight-lifter. You are 122 pounds and occasionally go bicycling.

HOWEVER! Can he lift weights with his eyeballs to strengthen them, or with his nose to make it impervious to a fast hard jab? Can you imagine him working a universal gym with his Adam's apple? Can he lift weights with his testicles to make them insensitive to a knee in the groin? Obviously not.

Those are vulnerable targets: eyes, nose, throat, groin. Those and others cannot be strengthened significantly enough to make them attackproof. So if you're attacked, don't try to pull away—it's too easy for him to hang on to you. Don't beat on his chest à la Scarlett O'Hara—he's got a lot of armor there. For us to get whopped in the chest is painful because of our breasts; all that men have there is muscle and heavy, springy bone underneath. Go instead for his nose, his testicles, his knees—some vulnerable target.

In addition to the vulnerable target/effective technique combination, remember two other things you have going for you: your adrenalin and his expectations. Any time you get frightened or angry or caught in an emergency, your body floods with adrenalin. This is a completely automatic reaction, and will give you "the strength of ten." So in addition to your muscular strength, you'll be getting a lot of help from your body's natural chemistry.

Also remember what the rapist's expectations are. He is expecting a victim; someone who will submit either with no struggle at all or with an ineffective struggle. He's looking for a victim, not a fight. Let that expectation work for you. If he's been foolish enough to mistake you for a victim, don't warn him otherwise until you're in a position to incapacitate him. For heaven's sake, don't tell him you "know self-defense" or you "have a black belt." He probably won't believe you, and he'll certainly take it as a challenge. Just wait for your opening, and *then* let him know what a dreadful mistake he's made.

The third component of successful self-defense is trusting your radar. Just like animals, we have an early warning system that makes us aware of danger. However, we rarely pay enough attention to the signals. We should. _

When you're in a situation in which you feel uncomfortable, *pay attention.* Your body may be trying to tell you something. If you're walking down the street at dusk and you hear footsteps behind you getting closer and closer, and it's making you uneasy, *pay attention.* Don't tell yourself that you're being paranoid and nothing's going to happen to you. It may be nothing *is* going to happen to you, but being uneasy at sound approaching from behind at dusk isn't paranoia, it's common sense.

It's best to turn around and face whatever's making you nervous, for several reasons. One is that nothing is ever gained by running away from our fears. Maybe those footsteps belong to somebody who's going to give you an odd look as he passes by, but so what?

If the person behind you or sidling up to you or approaching you in whatever fashion is a potential rapist, he may be deterred by the very fact that you stood straight and faced him instead of shrinking away. A straight back, strong stance, and level gaze are not "victim signals." But even if he doesn't recognize you as a non-victim, if you're facing him, at least you'll see him coming. And believe me, defending yourself against somebody coming at you from the front is far easier than getting rid of an attacker who's jumped on your back.

There is one final requirement, without which you will probably be unable to take advantage of either your adrenalin or his surprise; without which the techniques described here are next to useless, and that requirement is PRACTICE. If all you do is read this book and lay it aside, and neither think about nor practice the techniques, then you should have spent the money for something else.

It is important to think about what *you would do.* That is being prepared. Worrying about what might get done *to you* is being paranoid.

Remember that the techniques described in this book are ingredients, not recipes (no situation is ever exactly like any other). These moves are possibilities that can be adapted to whatever the immediate needs are. They are not some kind of self-defense true faith that must be adhered to rigidly. Where we show a kneecap stomp, for instance, you may find that your particular situation requires a smash to the nose. The techniques are not gospel. What *is* gospel is that you be totally committed in carrying out whichever you need.

Keeping those three things—totally committed response, effective-target technique, and radar—in mind, let's look at these two scenes.

1. A woman is waiting for the bus. A man walks up who is apparently also

waiting for the bus, but he keeps looking at her, and edging closer. This makes her nervous but she tells herself she's being silly. She's very nervous, but she doesn't say anything or move away. She looks in the opposite direction, still telling herself that she's just being paranoid and there must be something the matter with her to think that this perfectly nice man might be threatening to her. At this point, the perfectly nice man grabs her by the wrist and starts to pull her toward some bushes. She tries to pull away. When he doesn't let go, she hits him on the arm. He still doesn't let go and she hits him on the shoulder. He becomes annoyed and slugs her in the head, stunning her. He then drags her into the bushes and rapes her.

2. The scene is the same. When the man starts to stare at this woman and sidle toward her, she also is nervous. She tells herself that she does not like the non-verbal messages she's getting from him *at all*. She steps away. He again moves closer. She says to herself that the situation is feeling very threatening, and she had better be prepared. She steps away again, this time making sure that the way she is standing is firm and balanced. Instead of looking the other direction, she looks straight at the man. When he reaches to grab her arm, she isn't caught by surprise; she's seen it coming. The moment he grabs and pulls, she begins yelling —not screaming, but roaring like a lion. Instead of trying to pull her arm away, she steps forward and smashes her assailant in the nose with her free hand. Still roaring, she stomps to his kneecap. By now he has let her go, and she runs to safety, having hurt him badly enough that all he can think about is his pain.

In the second scenario, the woman listened to her radar and prepared herself. When the attack came, her response was an effective one, a combination of commitment and technique, and she got away. She got away because she was able to effectively injure her attacker.

V

Weapons and Targets

The only weapon that is always ready for use is one you never have to reach for. Consider:

Do you *always* carry your keys between your knuckles?

Do you *always* have a credit card or comb in your hand?

Do you *always* carry a can of repellent spray and keep your finger on the push button?

Of course not.

In any case, would scratching a rapist's face with a credit card or key really stop him, or would it simply infuriate him? And where will you aim the repellent spray if he grabs you from behind?

There are many problems with artificial weapons. One is that you're stuck if they fail, and there is a very good chance they won't work. For instance, many women carry cans of hair spray or perfume to use like mace. But they work only at very close range and only if the wind's in the right direction. What happens if he's too far away or the wind blows the spray in *your* face?

Another problem is the very real possibility that the rapist may take the weapon away and use it against his victim. This is particularly true with knives and guns. A gun or a knife should *never* be carried unless you are trained in its use and willing to use it.

The biggest problem, however, has to do with getting to the weapon in the first place. Even if you are a crack shot and are completely willing to use your weapon, if you have to fumble in your purse for it, you probably won't get a chance to use it. Or what will you do when he appears in the kitchen doorway and your pistol is in the basement where you were cleaning it?

The usefulness of a weapon depends on its effectiveness and its availability. So it's better not to depend on a weapon, which may not work or may not be there when you need it.

Depend instead on your body. You never have to reach for your fist; it's always right there at the end of your arm. We are, when the need arises, walking arsenals. Much of the body can be used as a weapon, singly or in combinations. Figure 1 points out the obvious weapons you have at your disposal.

Some weapons work better at long range; others are short-range weapons.

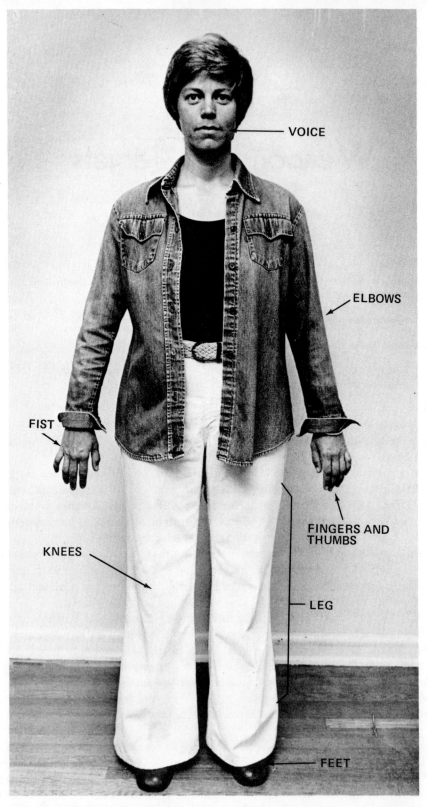

VOICE

ELBOWS

FIST

FINGERS AND
THUMBS

KNEES

LEG

FEET

FIGURE 1. Above, are things you take for granted about yourself, but they can serve as weapons for self-defense.

Teeth, for instance, are obviously short range. The legs, at the other extreme, have the longest reach.

Just as the range varies, so does effectiveness. The variation in effectiveness may be due to inherent factors, or it may be due to the way the weapon is used. Teeth have a very limited self-defense usefulness. If he has his hand over your mouth, you could certainly bite him, but a smashed nose is far more likely to stop him than a mangled finger. Probably the only situation in which teeth are truly useful is if he has forced you into oral sex. In that case, a good hard bite will disable him quite thoroughly.

Effectiveness may also be limited by improper use. For instance, fingers can be used both effectively—to gouge the eyes—or ineffectively—to scratch the face. One will stop him, the other won't.

Stance

The way you stand is as important as the techniques you use. Maybe it's more important, because a strong stance will support you, whereas a weak one will detract from your strength and balance. Also the way you stand gives out messages about your assertiveness and your willingness and ability to take care of yourself. Consider the different impression you get about the woman who is standing in Figure 2 as compared to Figure 3. Whenever you find yourself in a threatening situation, immediately take the kind of stance illustrated by Figure 3. The feet are approximately shoulder width apart, and one foot is slightly ahead of the other. This gives you balance and firm support for whatever technique you use, but is not so "rooted" a stance that you can't move quickly out of it. Figure 4 is an example of a stance that will give you equal support and balance, but is awkward to move out of. Also that stance will warn your attacker that you're ready for him, and you want whatever you do in response to his attack to come as a surprise. Remember, it's to your advantage that he thinks you're helpless.

Also note that in Figure 3 the back is straight, the shoulders are back, and the gaze is level and direct.

Voice/Kiai

The first weapon in your arsenal is your voice. Your voice is your first line of defense and is *always* used. Whatever striking or stomping techniques you use to get out of a hold, your "attack" starts with your voice.

Using your voice as a weapon is very different from using it to scream for help. If you're shrieking "Help, Help!" you are reinforcing the concept of yourself as a victim both in the rapist's mind and in your own mind. You are saying you cannot get out of this situation without someone coming to help you.

Consider, however, what it does to both you and the attacker if what you hear is a lion's roar. It may startle him so thoroughly that he lets go of you and flees. Several women who've taken our workshops have reported back to us that they stopped an attack just by yelling. One woman was caught on her porch and

FIGURE 2

FIGURE 3

FIGURE 4

slammed against the wall; she said she didn't have time to do anything else. The yell will usually require a "companion technique," however—a fist in the nose, a kick to the knee, etc.

The word for your battle cry is "kiai," a Japanese word with two components. Ki (pronounced *key*) means energy, power, strength, force, both personal and universal. Ai (pronounced *eye*) means to harmonize, bring together, unite. So Kiai means bringing together, uniting, all your force, your power, your strength and putting it into a vocal expression of energy.

To make kiai, pick a low sound, like "aah" or "oh" or a lion's roar, "raaarh." Stay away from "eee" or "hie" sounds. You want a deep, low, harsh roar instead of a shriek. Kiai comes from the diaphragm area, not the throat. Bring the sound up from your belly, open your mouth and throat wide, grow fangs and roar—"YAAAAHHH!!"

If you find your throat feels scratchy, or you start to cough, you have not opened up your throat. Think of having a comfortable tongue depressor in your mouth. It will help you open your throat. If you feel too inhibited to look fierce and roar like a lion, visualize a rapist standing in front of you, about to grab. Also, practice with a friend and have kiai contests.

In a real-life situation, be sure to wait until you've actually been attacked to kiai. Remember the scene at the bus stop—the woman didn't start to kiai when the man was sidling toward her, she waited until he grabbed her arm. If you warn an attacker with your kiai, he may panic and grab harder and stronger.

Hands

The hands have five striking or gouging surfaces: palm heel (Figure 5), front fist (Figure 6), top and bottom "hammerfist" (Figures 7, 8), fingers and thumb (Figure 9). The hand can also be used for a groin grab (Figure 10) which is highly effective, particularly at very close range, when there's no room to swing.

It is crucial for you to realize that effectiveness does not depend on brute strength. The power in a strike comes from speed and commitment, not the striker's ability to lift 300 pounds with one hand. You can demonstrate this to yourself very simply: Push on your nose as hard as you can. That's uncomfortable and probably hurts a little, but doesn't do any real damage. Now, take the heel of your hand and hit your nose in an upward motion.

Naturally you did that very lightly and probably slowly. Imagine, however, that you had hit an attacker's nose, the same way, only as fast and as hard as you could. You'd have hurt him very badly, badly enough for you to get away, not because of muscular strength, but because of a fast hard strike directed to a vulnerable target.

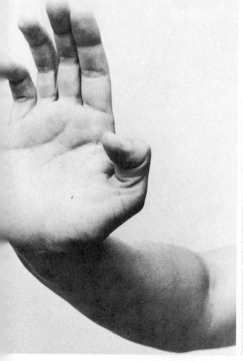

FIGURE 5

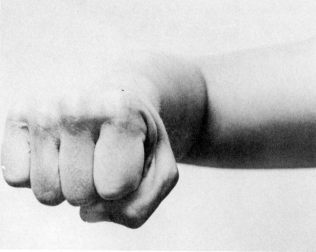

FIGURE 6

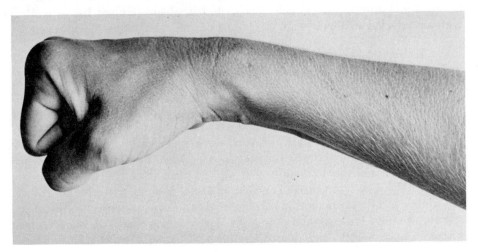

FIGURE 7

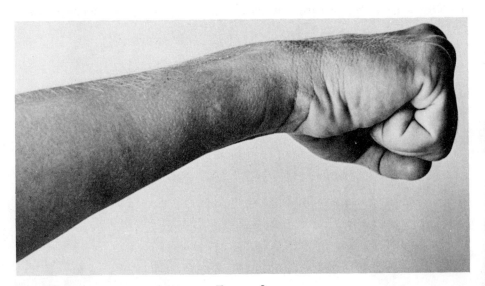

FIGURE 8

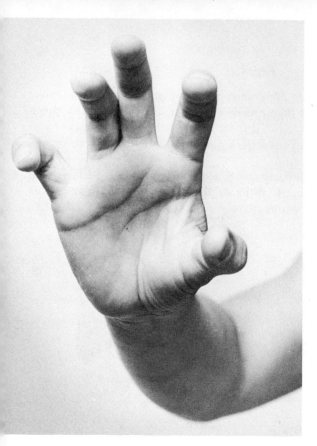

FIGURE 9

FIGURE 10

Legs

Your legs are, in some ways, your most powerful weapon. For one thing, they have several times the strength of the arms. For another, they have nearly twice the reach of the arms (Figure 11). Also, it is far more likely that an attacker will restrain your arms and hands than your legs. You will probably have more opportunity to use your legs than your arms.

The leg can also be divided into components according to contact surface. The knee and the foot can be used either to dislocate the rapist's knee or to stomp his instep as part of a hold-breaking combination.

FIGURE 11

Targets

Perhaps even more important than knowing what your weapons are is knowing what to do with them—what targets to use them against. You may have a devastating strike, but if you hit his shoulder instead of his groin, it probably won't damage him enough to stop him. Remember—again—that your goal is to inflict enough pain on the rapist that you can get away. Therefore, you must use your strength against his weakest points. Figure 12 illustrates the vulnerable targets. Forget the arms as targets. Forget the area marked by the x. It's the most heavily armored portion of the body. It's protected with bones and heavy muscle wall. The most vulnerable targets are the nose, the groin, the knees, the eyes, and the neck.

All of those targets are, more or less, equally efficient as pain conductors. That is, a good hard whack to the nose is just about as efficient as a slam into the groin, and both are not much less painful—in the short run anyway—than a stompkick to the knee.

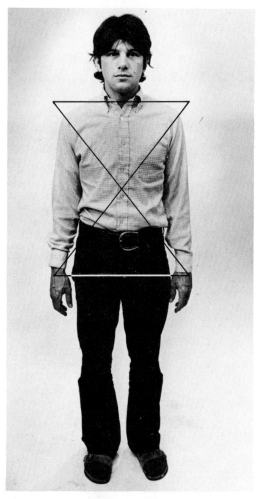

FIGURE 12

What you choose as a target depends on the situation. For instance, your choice may depend on which weapon you have free. If he's holding your arms, that means your weapons are your legs, and you're not going to try to kick his nose. You go for his knee instead.

Your choice may depend on how much distance there is between you. If he has his arms around your waist and is holding you against him, you're probably too close to kick his knee effectively and the nose or the groin would be a better target. Your choice may depend on whether he's grabbed you from the front, the side, or the back.

VI

Using Your Weapons

ARM AND HAND TECHNIQUES

In using your arms and hands as weapons, strike or stomp *through* the target, not *to* it. If you strike *to* the target, you will tend to stop the force of your blow too soon. If your target is his nose, don't just hit his nose, aim through his nose to the back of his head.

Always strike or stomp as fast and as hard as you can. Speed increases power —the faster you strike, the heavier the impact will be. Also, a slow strike can be easily caught or blocked. *Always look at your target!*

PALM-HEEL STRIKE

Extend your arm straight out in front of you. Now turn your hand up as if you were gesturing to someone to stop, or like a football player's stiff-arm. The fingers can be either held straight, or slightly curled. The contact surface is the heel of the palm only, not the whole hand.

To execute the strike, bring your hand to shoulder lever (Figure 13) and thrust

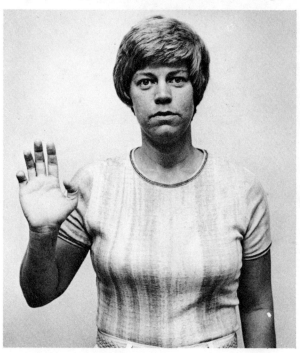

FIGURE 13

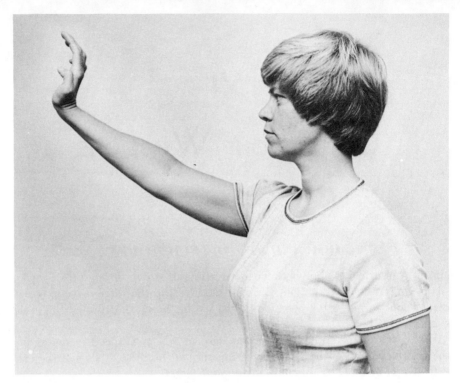

FIGURE 14

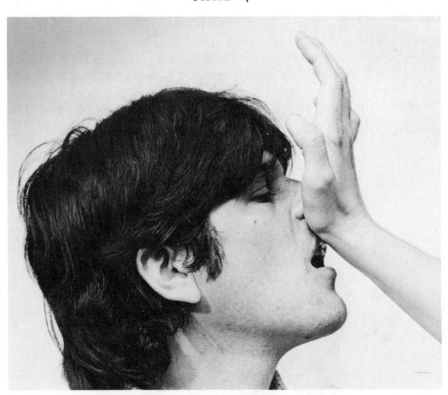

FIGURE 15

it straight forward, fast and hard (Figure 14). Aim the strike slightly upward.

Your target is the nose. Strike to the underside of the nose so as to smash it upward and backward (Figure 15).

This is a very effective medium-to-short-range technique to use whenever you have one or both arms free. Being hit with a palm-heel strike is roughly equivalent to being struck by the slightly padded end of a two-by-four.

FINGER/THUMB GOUGE

Both of these techniques are for use in desperate situations, when you feel that you have no other options. Using the gouge will result in temporary and perhaps permanent blindness and should really be used only the most serious of situations.

The thumb gouge uses both hands. Simply put your hands on the side of his head and press the thumbs into the eyes, hard (Figure 16).

The finger gouge is for use when only one hand is free. Tense the muscles in your hand, stiffen the fingers, and thrust into the eyes (Figure 17). Don't just scratch—thrust hard. Also, don't use just two fingers, you may miss; use all four.

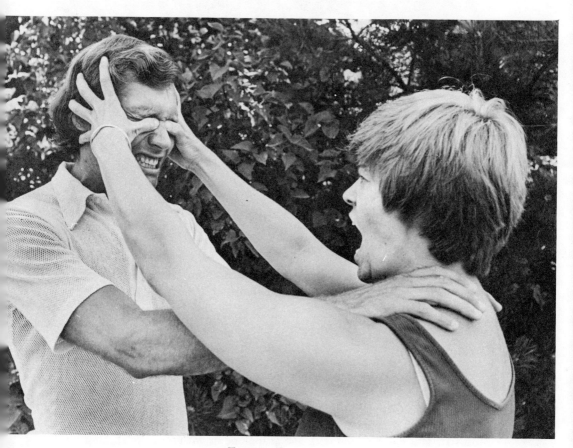

FIGURE 16

FIGURE 17

You will notice that in both of these illustrations, the rapist is choking the woman, certainly a life-threatening situation.

ELBOW SMASH

This is a very short-range technique, which is particularly useful in a confined space, such as in a car or sitting on a couch. Your targets are the nose, mouth, or Adam's apple. Bend the arm and raise it to the appropriate level (Figure 18). Then, keeping it bent, swing it forcefully into the nose or the Adam's apple (Figure 19). This can be done with one arm alone or with one arm striking the target and being given an additional push with the other arm.

Figure 18

Figure 19

The elbow smash is one of several techniques which will probably need to be followed by another. Because of the short range, it may be difficult to achieve enough speed and force in the blow to make it a "one-punch knockout."

DOUBLE-HAND STRIKE

The double-hand strike can be used at either short or medium range. Fold the hands, palms together, raise the arms and strike straight downward (Figure 20). Do not lace the fingers together. If you strike with your fingers laced, they will be crushed together from the force of the blow, and you'll hurt yourself as badly as you hurt him.

This is essentially a follow-up technique to be used in combination with some other strike or kick. Since the target is the back of the neck, obviously you will have had to do something else first that has caused him to double over so the back of his neck is exposed and within your reach.

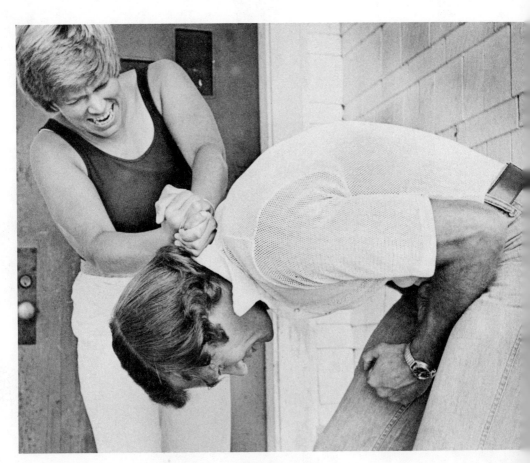

FIGURE 20

LEG TECHNIQUES

KNEE RAISE

How many times have we all heard, "If he gives you any trouble, just knee him in the crotch"? A knee in the crotch is probably the simplest technique available and probably causes the most pain for the least effort.

Unfortunately, men have heard about knees in the crotch as often as we have. Because they know how vulnerable the genitals are, men are lightning quick to protect the groin area. Also, they may be expecting you to try a knee to the groin and keep their legs together.

However, if your attacker has been helpful enough to spread his legs, simply raise the knee forcefully into his crotch (Figure 21). Ideally, he will be holding you close enough or you will have stepped forward and shortened the distance between you so that your leg comes up between his legs. The contact surface in this case is the top of your thigh, rather than the knee itself.

FIGURE 21

INSTEP STOMP

This is a technique that must *always* be followed with one or several other strikes and/or kicks. The usefulness of the instep stomp is in getting you out of a hold which is so confining that you can neither strike or kick effectively.

The target is the instep (top of foot). Simply raise your leg and stomp straight down, as hard as you can, onto the top of his foot (Figures 22, 23). It is best if you make contact with your heel, but the flat of the foot will also work.

FIGURE 22

FIGURE 23

Remember, this is not a "one-punch" technique. It will probably hurt him enough to get you out of a grab, but not enough to stop him. You will have to follow up with something else—a punch to the nose, a punch to the groin, a stompkick to the knee, whatever seems to be the most devastating at the time. But a stomp on the instep alone *won't* end the attack.

STOMPKICK

This is not a regular kick, since it doesn't involve any snapping from the knee. This is a stomp, which is directed out to the side instead of straight down.

I do not recommend trying to kick to the crotch—in fact, I recommend that you *don't* try a crotch kick. The reasons for this are several. One is the same as for the knee raise: Men are lightning quick to protect the groin. Another is that they may be expecting you to try a crotch kick and will be ready for it.

To execute the stompkick, raise the leg so it is *at least* parallel to the ground. The lower part of the leg should be angled outward (Figure 24). Now, stomp

FIGURE 24

straight out and slightly down, (Figure 25). *There is no back and forth snapping action.* This technique is simply a forceful straightening of the entire leg, exactly as in the instep stomp, except that instead of stomping downward, you are stomping out to the side.

The target is, obviously, the knee. Your contact surface is the flat of the foot. Ideally, you would contact his knee cap with the arch area of your foot, but this is such a powerful technique that you have a certain margin for error. Even if you don't stomp squarely on the knee, if you contact a little above or a little below, it will still work. Be careful, however, not to angle your stomp downward too much

FIGURE 25

or you'll make contact too low to do any damage (Figure 26). The stomp is directed more out to the side than downward. Remember that even if you cannot actually see his knee, it'll almost always be halfway between his feet and his crotch.

To aid in keeping your balance when using leg techniques, always bend your supporting leg slightly. That will give you more flexibility and spring than if you keep the leg straight.

When using the stompkick, as well as bending the supporting leg, counterbalance by leaning slightly to the side away from your kicking leg, as in Figure 25. If you're stompkicking with your right leg, lean your upper body a little bit to the left, and vice versa. Trying to keep your body completely upright will make balancing difficult.

Actually, in terms of balance, your body will take care of itself. You'll only feel really teetery when you're first learning the techniques. After you practice them, the problem should solve itself.

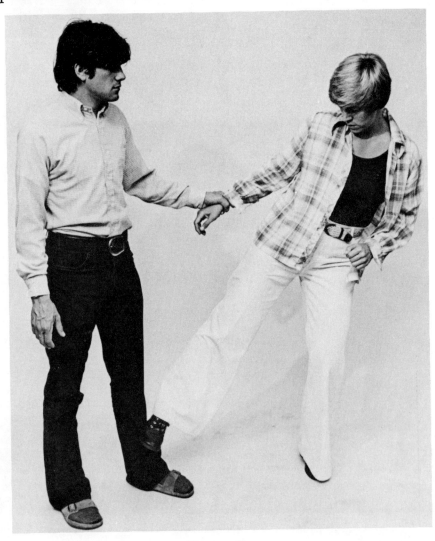

FIGURE 26

If you continue to feel seriously off balance, analyze what you're doing, find the problem, and correct it. Balance problems are usually caused by: (a) being stiff instead of flexible, (b) leaning forward when you should be standing straight, (c) leaning in the wrong direction, (d) all or several of the above.

FRONT SNAP KICK

Again, your target is the knee. Lift the leg so that it's about parallel with the ground (Figure 27). Now snap the knee straight forward (Figure 28) and then retract it quickly (Figure 29). The retraction is so your leg won't get caught. Don't "wind up," as in Figure 30. That will warn him that you're getting ready to kick, and he'll dodge or try to catch your foot—and maybe succeed.

There is no hip action in this kick as there is in the stompkick. The action here is all snapping back and forth from the knee joint. If you're wearing shoes, it doesn't matter what you do with your toes. If you're barefoot, try to make the kicking surface the ball of your foot by stretching your toes back toward your ankle (Figure 31).

FIGURE 27

FIGURE 28

FIGURE 29

FIGURE 30

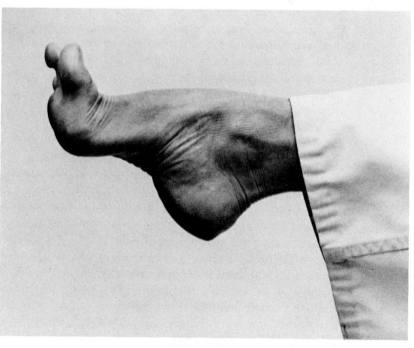

FIGURE 31

VII

Fighting Back

You have now learned basic techniques. These can be put into a variety of combinations. Some of them can be used singly as "one-punch" techniques, although a combination is almost always more effective.

This chapter shows some ways to put your basics together. These are some *possible* responses. They are responses that are simple and effective, but they certainly aren't the only ones.

What's important is not so much *what* you do as *how* you do it. Successful self-defense is a combination of:

1. Absolute commitment
2. Effective technique
3. Vulnerable target

To review:

Some targets are vulnerable, others are not. His weakest points are eyes, nose, neck, groin and knees. Forget the arms and the torso as target areas. Going for the arms, shoulders, or torso is a total waste of your energy. Don't "telegraph." Let your response come as a complete surprise to him.

All responses are accompanied by a kiai that continues until you're free. Strike or stomp through, not at, the target. You are actively fighting back, not just struggling.

Grabs

Surprisingly, there are a limited number of ways that you can get grabbed. To begin with, you can only get grabbed from the front, either side, or the back. (I'm leaving out the off-chance that he really has dropped out of a tree.) What weapon/target combination you use will depend on how he's approached you.

A general rule in getting out of holds and grabs is that simply breaking away isn't sufficient. You have to do something that will stop your attacker as well. Thus, if he grabs you by both wrists, it is simple enough to break that hold. But if that's all you do, he'll simply grab you again, and this time he'll grab harder and will be more committed to hanging on.

However, if you can damage your attacker without breaking a hold first, why not do so? Why take two steps when you can accomplish your goal in one? Particularly with several specific holds, I look upon the grab as a help. He's helping hold me up while I take him out. Of course, this isn't always so—sometimes you may have to break the hold first before you will be able to injure him. But when you can injure and break free simultaneously, you should do so. Certainly, you don't *ever* want to get into a pull-push kind of tussle. That becomes a contest of strength, which is too easy for you to lose.

FRONT/SIDE WRIST GRAB

He has grabbed you by the wrists. Don't try to pull away. Turn your body slightly at the same time raising your leg (Figure 32), and execute a stompkick to the knee (Figure 33). At the same time, grab him back. That may mean simply turning your hands over. Or, if he's wearing long sleeves, grab them. As soon as you stomp to the knee, pull him forward, hard, so he falls to the ground (Figure 34). You can follow through with a stomp to the crotch, if it seems necessary.

If he's grabbed only one wrist, you can follow the same sequence—turn, grab back, stompkick, pull down—or you can step forward and hit him with a palm-heel strike to the nose (Figure 35). This combination also works if he's grabbed your arm from the side (Figures 36, 37); here, you don't need to turn your body before kicking.

FIGURE 32

FIGURE 33

FIGURE 34

FIGURE 35

FIGURE 36

FIGURE 37

If he not only grabbed your arm(s) but is pulling you toward him, go with the pull. That's the last thing he expects; because he's leaning away from you, when you go with him, it'll throw him off balance, which is definitely to your advantage.

You have much more control over the situation when you control the movement. In those couple of seconds that he's off balance, you can regain your own and utilize whatever techniques seem most effective.

If he's pulling you along too fast for you to do anything effective, you'll have to break the hold. Reach through his arms and grab your own hand (Figure 38).

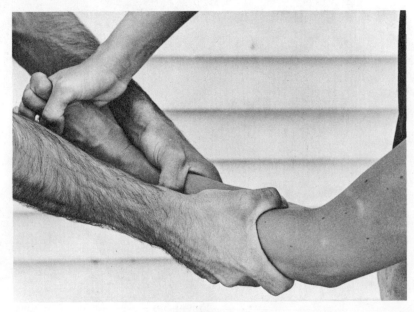

FIGURE 38

Then pull your arm toward you with a fast, snapping motion, initiated from the elbow (Figures 39, 40). To understand the motion, extend your arm in front of you and then, bending it at the elbow, bring your hand back to your chest. That's the motion you want for breaking this grab—it's a snap from the elbow. Your other arm just helps it along. Follow through with a stompkick.

FIGURE 39

FIGURE 40

HAIR GRABS

Hair pulling is an old and painful fighting technique which is sometimes used in an assault situation. Before you can respond to the attack, you will probably have to neutralize your own pain.

If you have long hair, you can ease the pain by grabbing your own hair between the attacker's hand and your scalp (Figure 41). Follow through with your free hand (Figure 42).

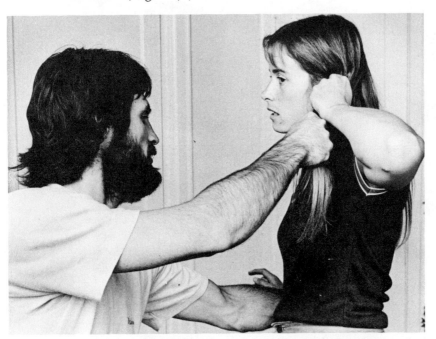

FIGURE 41

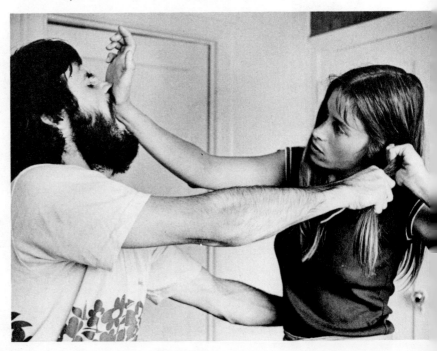

FIGURE 42

FIGURE 43

If you have short hair, clamp both your hands over the attacker's hand and press down firmly (Figure 43). Here your follow through will most likely require a leg technique (Figure 44).

FIGURE 44

CHOKE HOLDS

Being choked is, for many of us, one of our worst fears. The thought of hands around our throats brings on cold sweat and feelings of panic. Much of this fear of being choked has to do with the fear of not being able to breathe—of drowning out of the water, so to speak. But the damage from choking comes not so much from no breath in the lungs as no blood in the brain—at least initially.

Because being choked is so frightening, most of us never think about how long we can go without breathing. Find a watch or clock with a second hand, and time how long you can hold your breath. Everyone should be able to hold a breath for at least fifteen seconds. (If you can't either you're not really trying or you should see a doctor). You may be slightly gaspy if you held your breath for a long time, but you can see that you're in no danger of collapsing. So it's not being unable to breathe that makes being choked hard dangerous.

The danger and damage comes from the lack of blood flow to the brain. The brain receives almost all its blood supply from the carotid arteries, which run parallel to the windpipe. If you are being choked hard, the carotids will be pinched off—blood can't get through—and you'll pass out. It takes at least five seconds of very hard choking to make you pass out.

But: It takes two-tenths of one second to do a thumb or finger gouge into the eyes. It takes seven-tenths of one second to stompkick to the knee. It takes five-tenths of one second to do a little finger pull and break the choke.

In any case, many rapists use a choke hold, not to actually choke their intended victim but to frighten her into submission. Your response to a choke hold should take into consideration how hard his grip is. If he's exerting all his strength, that's the time to use a thumb gouge (see Figure 16). But if, as does happen, he just has his hands around your neck and is squeezing lightly, another technique may do as well.

FIGURE 45

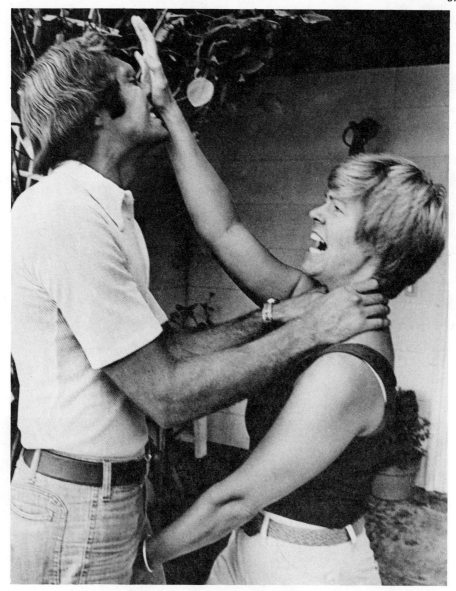

FIGURE 46

If he's choking you that his arms are almost in a circle, he'll be fairly close to you and you can come up between his arms with a palm-heel strike to the nose (Figure 45), or you can do a double: palm heel to the nose and hammerfist to the groin (Figure 46). If he's holding his arms close together, go around them on the outside, and use both hands (Figure 47). If he's enough taller than you that to try to strike to the nose or the eyes is impossible, go for the groin instead, with a groin pull (Figure 48).

If he has long arms and is holding you away from him so you can't get to the face area, go for the knee. Grab his wrists, turn your body slightly, and do a stompkick to the knee (Figure 49).

FIGURE 47

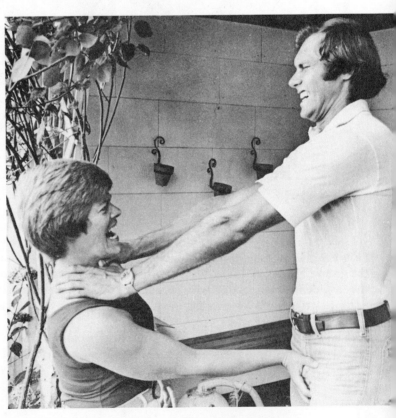

FIGURE 48

FIGURE 49

If he's knocked you down and is straddling you and his face area is in range, do a thumb or finger gouge, depending on whether you have one or both hands free (see Figure 17). If he's leaning away so you can't reach his face, do a groin pull (Figure 50).

FIGURE 50

CHOKES FROM BEHIND

If you're grabbed from behind, depending on how hard he's squeezing and how close his body is, you may have to break the hold before you can do any damaging technique. To break a rear choke, use a little finger grab.

Jam your thumbs up under his little fingers, between your neck and his hands (Figure 51). (This is a good deal less difficult than it sounds—almost all the gripping strength is in the thumb and first two fingers. The little fingers are relatively weak.) Grab the little fingers firmly with your entire hand and yank—*hard* —straight back (Figure 52). At the same time you're yanking, turn your body so

FIGURE 51

FIGURE 52

FIGURE 53

you're at least sideways to him. Now you can follow through with whatever technique or combinations you want: stompkick or palm-heel strike (Figures 53, 54), to mention two possibilities. But you have to follow up with something to stop him. Just breaking the choke hold isn't enough.

As a general rule, because the pressure of a choke can be increased so quickly and so dangerously, it is probably better to break the hold first, then injure the

FIGURE 54

rapist. There are, of course, possible techniques if you choose not to break the hold, but these depend on his not choking you hard, and holding you fairly close to him.

One possibility is to step slightly to one side and do a rear hammerfist into the groin (Figure 55). Another is to do a back kick to the knee (Figure 56). A third is a groin pull. However, each of these techniques will probably need to be followed up with something else.

Remember, a choke hold has the greatest damage potential of any kind of grab, and can justify the most devastating response. No sane person would feel happy about blinding someone, but the choice may be between your life or his sight. For me, the choice is uncomfortable but clear: my life.

FIGURE 55

FIGURE 56

BEAR HUGS

A bear hug somewhat reduces your options, since your arms are restrained, although you may be able to use them anyway. But you still have your legs.

You're grabbed from the front, and your arms are pinned to your sides. Likely, given that he's probably a little taller than you, your arms are free from the elbow down. Simply move your arm forward slightly and execute a groin pull (Figure 57).

If he's helpful enough to have his legs apart, a knee raise is the best possible defense (Figure 21). Or, if you can't move your arms, stomp hard to his instep and swing outward with your arms at the same time (Figure 58). Of course, you must then follow through with something else—a stomped instep will be sufficiently painful to make him loosen his hold enough for you to break it, but not enough to stop him altogether. *Follow through*—you have both arms and legs free now.

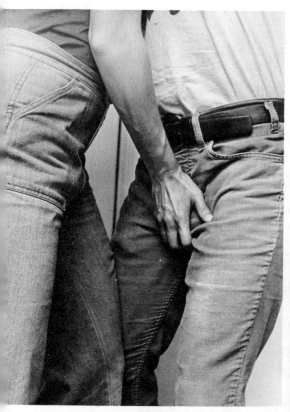

Figure 57

Figure 58

FIGURE 59

With a rear bear hug, you can again use a groin pull, followed by a knee raise to the face when he doubles over (Figures 59, 60). Or, you can do a back kick

FIGURE 60

FIGURE 61

(Figures 61, 62) or an instep-stomp breakaway. But with both the back kick and the instep stomp you have only gotten out of the hold—you then have to follow through.

FIGURE 62

FIGURE 63   FIGURE 64

If he has you pinioned from the rear, with one arm around your neck and one of your arms twisted behind your back (Figure 63), you have pretty much the same set of possibilities as with a rear bear hug. To take some of the pressure off the throat, simply lean back slightly and turn slightly toward his elbow (Figure 64). (Turning away from the elbow will increase the pressure.) Then use the groin pull or a back kick and follow through, or an instep stomp and follow through, or whatever you devise when practicing that works for you.

Ground/Prone Techniques

You wake up in the middle of the night, for no apparent reason, but you sense something. Then you see a dim figure across the room. He moves toward the bed with his hands outstretched. You are paralyzed with fear (Figure 65). Isn't that one of our worst rape nightmares?

But let's run through it again. You wake up in the middle of the night and the dim figure is moving toward you. Instead of being paralyzed, you free your legs and thrust kick into his groin (Figure 66). As he doubles over in pain, you smash his nose with a palm-heel strike.

Or you wake up to find his hands around your throat. You gouge his eyes, grab his head and swing him over onto the bed, and do a hammerfist to the groin (Figures 67, 68, 69). Then you get up and call the police.

Obviously if you're in bed, or have been knocked to the ground, your options are somewhat fewer than if you're still on your feet. But "fewer" is not the same as "none"

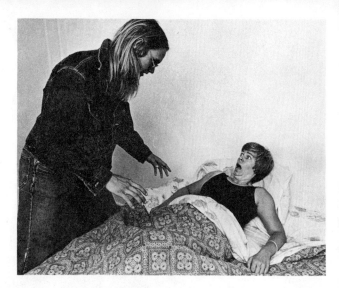

FIGURE 65

FIGURE 66

FIGURE 67

FIGURE 68

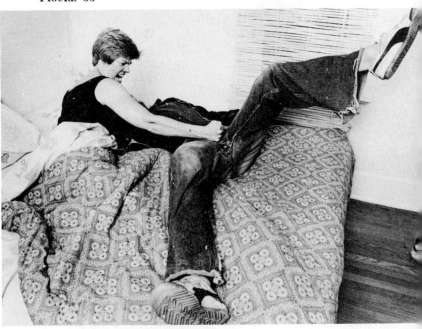

FIGURE 69

If the rapist has grabbed you and is falling with you, try first of all to thrust with your feet and/or twist your body in such a way that you fall with as much of your weight *on him* as possible. Even if you're quite small, it'll help. A hundred pounds landing on *anybody's* stomach is bound to knock a little wind out of them. If both your arms are pinned, the split second you hit the ground (hopefully on top of him) roll and twist so you get at least one hand free. Then you can use a finger gouge to the eyes, or a palm heel to the nose, or a groin pull, to name three logical possibilities (Figures 70, 71, 72).

FIGURE 70

FIGURE 71

FIGURE 72

If he has pushed you, go with the direction of the push and try as you're fall-ing to put as much distance between you and your attacker as possible. (You'll probably stagger a few steps before you go down.) Twist as you go down so you land on your back. If you land on your side or stomach flip onto your back im-mediately, then raise your legs into position for a thrusting kick. Kick straight forward into the groin (Figure 73). Or you can kick to the knee (Figure 74). This kind of kick is a straight thrusting motion—much the same as the stompkick. Don't flail your legs as if you were riding a bicycle. Once you've con-nected with the kick, leap to your feet. If you've hit the groin hard enough, you won't need to do anything else; otherwise follow through with whatever tech-nique seems appropriate.

If he's knocked you down and is straddling you, use a hand technique to the face or groin and then thrust with the hips and roll him off. To push him off, bend your knees to give yourself leverage and thrust up and to one side with your hips and torso. Then follow through with a "finish" technique (Figures 75, 76, 77).

FIGURE 73

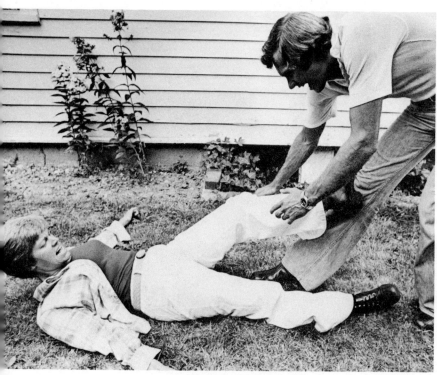

FIGURE 74

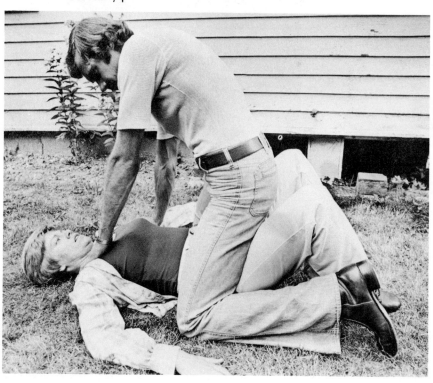

FIGURE 75

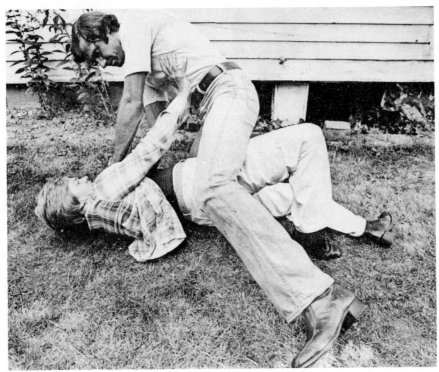

FIGURE 76

FIGURE 77

Conclusion

The above situations are a number of attacks and response possibilities. As I've said, they aren't the only ones possible, although you'll find in practice that the kinds of responses are double or triple the kinds of attacks. The number of ways to get grabbed really is far more limited than any of us think.

One thing to keep in mind is that an immediate response is almost always better than a delayed response. However, if you are attacked and grabbed in such a fashion that there simply is no possible immediate response (Figure 78), don't panic. Wait for an opening.

In Figure 78, I don't really see any truly workable way out. Even an attempt at a back kick to the knee won't work because his knee is out of range. But consider, can he rape me while we're in that position? Obviously not. At the very least, setting aside the awkwardness of the position, we both still have our clothes on. He's going to have to let go with at least one hand to tear my clothes away and unzip his own pants. That's what I'm waiting for, and all I need. So if you're grabbed in a way that you can't get out of, just wait. There will almost always be an opening for you to use. If it's impossible for you to respond, most probably it's impossible for him to rape you.

Another option is for you to act as if you think the whole thing is wonderful. Many men *really believe* that all women secretly want to be raped. If you pretend to go along with his program, it might just confirm what he always thought and put him off guard. The catch is that it's you who's really in control, not him. This is a particularly useful way of dealing with the situation if he's using a weapon.

FIGURE 78

I have not dealt with any of the various ways to physically disarm an attacker who's using a weapon, because I believe that those techniques are next to impossible to learn from a book. Unless you've learned those techniques directly from a teacher, your best defense is verbal. Convince him to put his weapon aside. In many, if not most cases, he's using the weapon for its scare value. If you convince him you're frightened and that you'll go along with him, probably he'll put his gun or knife or other weapon down. Whatever you're saying is just a ploy to put him off guard. When your opening comes, you must follow through instantly. He'll probably still be unconscious when the police arrive.

Remember, it's not so much what you do as that the response you make is completely committed and uses an effective technique directed to a vulnerable target.

VIII

Practicing

Remember what was said before: If you simply read about these techniques, think "yeah, that looks like it'd work," but never think about or actually practice them, you probably should have bought something else with the money you spent on this book.

Successful self-defense is a matter of preparation—you can't pull it out of the hat like a magic rabbit. I'm not saying that in order to defend yourself, you need to spend years studying fancy techniques (or a martial art, which will be discussed later). I'm simply saying that it's a matter of preparation—which means practice.

There are two kinds of practice that are essential. One is the actual physical practicing of the moves. The other is playing "What-if Games"—mental practice.

Physical Practice

You should go over the physical techniques described here, and ones you make up yourself, on a regular basis. They can be done alone, with a friend, or better yet, a group of friends, say on a weekly basis. In group practice, you can come up with new techniques and variations of the ones here.

A word of warning: practicing with men can sometimes be more harmful than beneficial. There is a lot of ego tied up in a man's image of himself as strong (particularly compared with women) and unless you are sure that the man you want to practice with won't let that get in the way, practice with other women. It won't help your feeling about your ability to defend yourself if the man you're practicing with decides to "prove" that he's stronger and meaner than you are by grabbing you in a tight bear hug, refusing to let go, and then saying, "Ha, ha, you couldn't get out of that one."

You could have, of course, had you been willing to really stomp on his instep or yank his testicles, but he's (supposedly) your friend. So you wind up feeling there's no hope after all, just like you've been told all these years. Unless you're sure that the man you want to practice with won't indulge in that sort of silliness, practice with other women.

But whoever you practice with, practice often. You want the moves to come without thinking, automatically. They won't without practice. And practicing simply does not take that much time. A friend and I timed ourselves running through all the techniques with each of us being the attacker once and the defender once, and it took us eighteen minutes. We went straight through and didn't stop, but we didn't rush, either.

The more time you spend, the better and stronger you'll be, of course. But even though you needn't spend a lot of time, *you must spend some.* Ten minutes a day could save your life.

In terms of your physical practice, as well as going over the moves, you should practice actually making contact with an object. You can practice hitting and kicking the air until the millennium, but for the techniques to become real to you, you must really hit something.

All you need to practice making contact is an object to hit and either someone to hold it for you or something to prop it against. The object should be firm but not hard. Leave breaking bricks to the experts.

A thick couch cushion would be good, or a rolled-up sleeping bag, or even a pillow case stuffed with rags. If you want to get fancy, spend a couple of dollars at a surplus store for a duffle bag, the kind that has grommets and a prong on the top (not the kind you carry like a gym bag). Then fill it with rags, very firm foam rubber, or some other material you have available. I filled my bag with discarded retread backing from a local tire retreader's trash bin. It looks like silver cloth tape and makes a very good stuffing. Don't use a heavy and unyielding filling like sand. Your object is to make good contact, not sprain your wrist.

FIGURE 79

Once you have your object plus a friend, practice the hand and leg techniques learned in the weapons chapter. Have your friend hold the object at the appropriate level (prop it up if you're practicing alone) and whale away on it. Practice your kiai at the same time (warn your neighbors first). Remember to strike or stomp *through* the object, not *at* it (Figures 79–82).

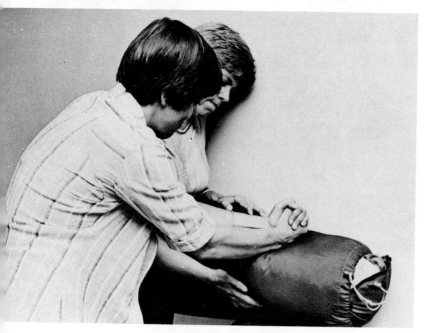

FIGURE 80

FIGURE 81

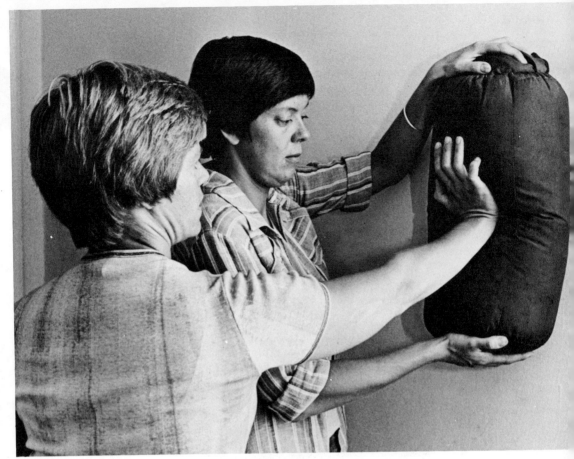

FIGURE 82

Mental Practice

The other form of practice is "what-if" games. There is an enormous difference between being prepared and being paranoid about an attack. Being prepared begins by saying to yourself, "What would I do if:

He tried to pull me into his car?

He tried to push me into an alley?

He showed up in my kitchen doorway and told me to take off my clothes?

He appeared in the back seat of my car?

He appeared standing over me at night while I was in bed and the kids were in the next room?"

Picture yourself in familiar situations—at home, at work, at school, going somewhere, waiting for the bus, whatever—then construct a plan for what you'd do if you got jumped. This is particularly important for those settings that have a potential for danger. Waiting for the bus, for instance, is more likely to be dangerous than sitting at your desk.

Examine the four situations illustrated in Figures 83–86. What would you do? The other form of mental practice is a companion to "what-if" games. It has to do with attitude. ALWAYS SEE YOURSELF WINNING!

FIGURE 83

FIGURE 84

FIGURE 85

FIGURE 86

IX

A Note About Clothing

Much has been said about a woman's clothing provoking rape. The problem with this myth is deciding what is provocative clothing. If we ask every man we know what he considers provocative dress, chances are we would get a different answer from every man. We can't agree on any one type of dress as universally provocative. Because most rape is planned and because the definition of what is provocative differs greatly from person to person, it is not likely that clothing is responsible for rape. Some men find fully clothed women most provocative.

Some women wear short skirts, tight sweaters, loose blouses, or low-cut tops for a specific reason. They like them and/or they are using them to meet men. In this country initiation of a relationship has been left to men, who can use very direct methods to secure sexual experience. Women have not had the same techniques available, so for many women clothing is a way of initiating contact. But it is important to remember that the woman still has the right to pick and choose her company. When she says no to someone, it should be respected. She may be asking to meet men, but she is not asking to be raped. Unless women walk around with a sign that says "Rape Me," they are not asking to be raped by the way they dress!

Our clothing *does* determine how well we can defend ourselves in a confrontive situation. We are not advocating that we all dress in jogging suits, constantly ready to do battle. What follows are a few aspects of dress you might want to consider before going into a vulnerable situation. You can greatly enhance your safety by dressing in a way that increases your mobility.

SHOES

Shoes are, perhaps, the most important aspect of your dress. Whatever shoes you wear, you must be able to keep them on while running or be able to get out of them quickly. Sandals and platform shoes are not good for this. You want to be able to run, keep your balance, and perhaps kick in the shoes you wear.

COATS AND SKIRTS

Check the mobility you have in a long coat or skirt. Are they so heavy that you can't move quickly? Are they so tight that you can't move very far? Remember, you may need to extend your leg for a kick, your arm for a strike, or simply run away. Be sure you can do this.

JACKETS AND BLOUSES

Some of the clothes we wear restrict movement when buttoned down. Can your arms fully extend? Can you lift your arms above your head to ward off a blow? Your arms need to be free for them to do what you need them to do.

JEWELRY

Protruding rings can be good edges when you make a fist. Scarves and necklaces (particularly whistles) are dangerous if they can be used to strangle you.

LONG HAIR

It is not uncommon for you to be grabbed by the hair during an attack. If you wear your hair under your sweater or jacket, it is less accessible.

PURSES

Purses with small straps carried in the hand are very vulnerable. Our first reaction in an attempt to steal the purse is to pull back. That can escalate the purse snatching into a war of wills. Shoulder strap purses worn between the body and the arm are less accessible. Thin straps can be cut by razor blades. A reinforced strap is better.

KNAPSACKS

If worn over both shoulders as they are meant to be, knapsacks can be pulled on from behind and the force of the pull will have you on the ground, still attached to your knapsack. If they are carried over one shoulder only, you can drop your shoulder (and knapsack) and run away.

The above are only some guidelines to enhance your safety and increase your ability to react effectively. They are not a dress code.

PART III

X

Studying a Martial Art

If you are interested in studying a martial art—which I fervently recommend—the following will give you some guidance. A martial art is not the same as self-defense. All the arts are based on the idea of self-defense, of course, but studying and training in an art goes far beyond learning how to dislocate a knee or smash a nose. In fact, if you do begin studying, you may wonder what any of it has to do with self-defense, and it may be a while before you really feel its relevance. I assure you, it's there.

The immediate benefits have to do with both body and mind. You will become stronger and more flexible. You will discover that almost without knowing it, your body is learning how to take care of itself without you telling it anything. Balance and movement improve.

Studying an art will also provide you with structure and some externally imposed discipline. You can say, "Well, I don't feel like going through these techniques tonight," and put this book away quite easily. But if you have a class to go to, particularly one you've paid for, you're much more likely to be disciplined.

Most important of all, you learn that you are *not* weak, *not* helpless, and you *are* able to take care of yourself. It's a beautiful feeling.

There are many different martial arts, and under the general heading of each art, there are many styles. It's much like religion—there's a church and an art for everybody's needs. Finding what's right for you will probably require some shopping around.

The following paragraphs are a very broad description of the unarmed martial arts. They are not meant to be anything more than a sketchy introduction.

The arts are initially categorized by their origin—Japanese/Okinawan, Korean, and Chinese. The more common Japanese/Okinawan arts are karate, aikido and judo. The best-known Korean art is Tae Kwon Do; hapkido has recently become known in the United States. The Chinese arts are the various styles of kung fu and tai chi. Actually, all the Asian unarmed martial arts have their origin in China.

The Japanese karate styles theoretically balance striking and kicking 50–50, although in practice, striking tends to be somewhat emphasized. The Korean styles, both in practice and theory, emphasize kicking over striking. The Chinese styles are also fairly evenly divided between striking and kicking. Judo and aikido teach throws and holds.

All the arts have their strong points and their weak points. Obviously, they all have more strong points than weak ones, or they would never have survived. Arguments such as, "Judo is better than karate and both are better than tai chi" or "Goju karate [my style] is better than Shorin karate [your style]" are silly. You can learn the same discipline and the same inner strength in all the arts and styles. They may be taught differently and called by different names, but in the end, they're the same—or should be. Lack of discipline and meaning is the instructor's fault, not the failing of the art.

Begin your search for the right art with the Yellow Pages in the telephone directory, under the heading "Judo/Karate Instruction." Then go and visit the schools. I recommend that you investigate a judo school, aikido school, several karate and kung fu schools, and a tai chi school. Take some time and expend some effort. It's an important decision.

Ask to talk to the instructor. Tell him or her (usually him) that you're interested in studying an art, and ask him to tell you about his art and particular style. Find out what the school's tuition policy is. Many schools require a contract. Many do not. (Personally, I can see the economic justification for contracts but don't like the idea. If you sign a contract, you'll have to pay, even if you drop the class after six weeks.) Ask to visit a class. If the instructor says you can't, go somewhere else. It's your time, your body, your money. You should be able to see what you're considering committing yourself to.

Once you get some feeling for which art you're interested in, look more closely at the position of women in the school. This is *particularly* important if you're interested in karate, kung fu, or the Korean styles. How many women are in the class? How many are at the higher ranks (brown and black belts)? If you know that the instructor's been teaching for eighteen years in the same spot and he currently has 150 students but only six female white belts (beginners), two orange belts (low intermediate), and one green belt (intermediate), *go somewhere else!*

The martial arts were a male domain until only recently and there are many schools where it is still impossible to be a woman and learn anything. The instructor may assure you that he thinks it's wonderful that women are getting into the arts, but look at his classes before you really believe him.

In the styles that fight in class, do the women fight? Or do they step aside and do something else? If they do fight, are they fighting with the men? If the women fight only with each other, that's a bad sign. If they do fight with the men, are they really fighting or just playing patty-cake? Those are some indicators of whether or not the instructor takes women seriously. And I can promise you, if the instructor doesn't take women seriously, nobody else will either—neither the other students nor yourself.

Best of all, talk to the other women students. They can tell you, both in what they say and don't say, how it is in that particular school.

In some communities, another option is studying at an all-women's school. There are many schools that are run strictly by and for women. There will be a smaller number of women's schools than traditional schools in any given location —for instance, in Seattle, there is one women's school and eighteen traditional schools. But if there is one in your area, you should certainly go there and see how it feels to you. Your local Women's Center or YWCA will probably know about it. Even if there's no women's school, one or some of the traditional schools may have classes just for women. But if that's the case, check the class out *very carefully*. Women-only classes in traditional schools are often less rigorous, the demands made of the women less serious, and the women in actuality are treated like second-class citizens.

But there are a number of advantages to studying in a women's school, one of which is not having to fight sexism, whether open or covered up, on the part of your male instructor and fellow students. Another advantage is the special kind of sisterhood and solidarity that can grow among women studying in a women's school. On the other hand, some women find the pressures of a traditional school, particularly in fighting, to be an advantage they value.

However, whether you study in a women's school or in a traditional school, you will, if you commit yourself, learn discipline, self-confidence, and a special kind of internal strength and peace.

XI

Studying Rape Prevention

Fortunately, there are many rape-prevention projects in existence around the country. They take many forms—brochures, community-relations police programs, films, classes in assertiveness and self-defense. The following information is based on what we've learned in the four years the Rape Prevention Forum has existed.

Obviously, the first step in preventing rape is an awareness of the problem—a function rape-crisis centers have admirably filled. But there also needs to be skill development going beyond awareness. Following are some guidelines for examining rape-prevention material that is available to you.

Brochures are the most popular method of distributing rape-prevention information, and almost every police department, rape-crisis center, crime-prevention program or insurance company has such literature. There are certain things to look for in an effective brochure.

First, it should not present itself as the entire answer. Common myths, local statistics and listings of local resources are good material for a brochure, but that information should not presume to prevent rape. There is a world of difference between awareness and prevention. Accurate statistics can help you avoid specific areas with a high incidence of sexual assault, but statistics will not defend you when confronted with a potential assault. If a brochure advertises prevention methodology, it should include specific responses to specific assault situations.

Brochures should be presented in a positive and constructive manner. We all hear the tips that say don't walk down dark streets, look in the back seat of your car, ask for identification, have your car keys ready. Those are excellent suggestions that should be integrated into our daily activities, but they have little impact on a large percentage of rapes. The material needs to go beyond listing a handful of situations that distract us from other forms of danger or give us a false sense of security—a belief that we will be safe if we only follow the guidelines given in the brochure.

It is vitally important that tips tell us what we *can* do as opposed to telling us what we can't or shouldn't do. For instance, the difference between "Don't carry heavy loads of groceries," and "Use a cart to carry groceries so that your hands and legs are free" is psychologically immense. One simply says don't; the other creates options—free hands for fighting back, unburdened body for running. Other examples are:

Don't rely on weapons for protection. They can be taken away from you and used against you.	If you use a weapon, be well-trained in its use and be willing to use it immediately.
Never leave a key under your doormat, in the mailbox or any other obvious place.	If you hide an extra key, place it in the dirt of a flower pot or other undetectable places.
Walk in well-lighted areas.	If you are out after dark, walk with someone else if possible. If alone, move strongly and quickly, constantly checking your surrounding environment.

We deserve to know more than long lists of what we *can't* do. Inclusion of constructive alternative actions assumes we are intelligent adult women rather than stupid children who need our activities limited "for our own good."

Common "safety tip" brochures can increase a woman's fear unjustifiably by giving her advice that limits her mobility. We can become so concerned about safety after dark, for example, that we never go out at night. We might develop a false sense of security about daylight hours and be caught off guard by the salesman who comes to the door during the day. We need, instead, ideas for how to maintain desired activities.

When there is a series of assaults on young women, school administrators often purchase brochures listing the type of tips we have been discussing. After distributing the material, they feel they have done their duty and no further information or skill development is provided. Tips not only need to be comprehensive and positive, they also need to be followed up with personal attention to the individual woman's needs. She needs increased options and responses to an assault situation.

Films, books, classes or brochures often emphasize reliance on others as a major prevention technique. This may mean screaming for help, always walking with a man or not living alone. This emphasis tends to weaken self-confidence and to be generally destructive of feelings of competence and self-reliance. And while they are not panaceas, self-confidence and self-reliance generate an attitude that frequently deters approaches.

When we do discuss a need for reliance on another person, we need to recognize that other people may not always be willing to help. The important question is, if other people fail to come, are we helpless?

Another very important issue is who are the people we are supposed to rely on to be safe? It is a cruel paradox to be told we are *only* safe with men, when rapists are always men. Actually, the presence of another woman or children can greatly decrease a woman's chances of becoming a victim. The assumption that the only person worth relying on is a man not only adds to our victimization, it prevents women from exploring many supportive roles for each other.

It also is crucial that rape-prevention material consider rape as many different crimes along a continuum. We make this point throughout this book. A full range of options is needed. Rapists vary in their individual motivations and in what type of violence they perpetrate. Therefore, one pat technique will never address all situations. We have seen a significant decrease in this mentality, but there still are some "experts" who believe they have the One Answer. Women often look for easy guarantees—one magic rule that guarantees safety. There are people ready to give such dangerous instruction, but remember, nothing is effective in every situation.

By the same token, if you are considering a class in prevention, you should check out the range of options being taught. Some rape-prevention classes only offer one technique and do not pretend to be comprehensive. Fine, but in that case, you may want to combine that class with one in assertiveness training and another in physical self-defense.

If you know a martial art, you still might not be able to be assertive to the man who insists on taking you home from the tavern because he bought you a couple of beers. There is no reason to let his advance go to the point where you must physically defend yourself. On the other hand, a very assertive attitude in daily activities doesn't mean you can get out of a surprise attack.

The sex of the teacher or author of rape-prevention material is something to consider. It is valuable to have women teaching other women. Male teachers and some women subscribe to the theory that treating the rapist "like a human being" will deter the attack. While this may work in some cases, it is certainly not always valid.

The theory makes some faulty assumptions. First, it assumes that the rapist is listening to you and genuinely cares about your feelings, your marital status, your health. Second, it assumes he is a reasonable, compassionate "good boy gone bad" who isn't very serious about what he's planning and can be easily distracted. One male author cites a story in which he tells of a woman starting a "meaningful relationship" which led to marriage because she treated her rapist "like a human being." It is obvious that a woman faced with rape is not being treated like a human being.

In the first part of this book we stress that rapists often test the victim to find how far she is willing to go in putting his feelings before her own. Treating a rapist like a human being is a dubious defense.

Much of the rape-prevention material available is not particularly helpful, but most of it is well intended. Susan Brownmiller analyzes the effects of such material in her book, *Against Our Will* (Simon and Schuster, 1975). On page 398, she states:

> By seeing the rapist always as a stranger, never one of their own, and by viewing the female as a careless, dumb creature with an unfortunate tendency to stray, they exhorted, admonished, and warned the female to hide herself from male eyes as much as possible. In short, they told her not to claim the privileges they reserved for themselves. Such advice, well intended, solicitous and genuinely concerned—succeeded only in further aggravating the problem, for the message they gave was to live a life of fear, and to it they appended the dire warning that the woman who did not follow the rules must be held responsible for her violation.

There is no double bind like this in any other kind of crime-prevention material. It is the lot of the potential rape victim to live in fear, afraid of the wrong things, with the certainty that "straying" will bring her immediate assault.

Studies prove that the behavior of men and women conforms to some degree to the expectations of those important to them. By insisting that women are incapable of self-preservation and are basically foolish, we insure that women will act in that manner. If we ever assumed that women are cautious, extremely capable and resourceful (which we are), we would likely see the contrived need for "safety tips" diminish.

To summarize, rape-prevention material should offer constructive alternatives to potentially threatening circumstances. It should stress self-reliance and address a variety of potential rape situations.

Your own personal needs will dictate other considerations. Add them. Demand the best of your training and education. You deserve it!

XII

Conclusion

All the options open to women for their response to sexual assault are not enough. The problem of rape is not the responsibility of women in America. While we can learn to insure our own individual safety, real prevention must be a community-wide action.

There are many elements that need to exist for an environment conducive to assault prevention. An individual woman can take precautions and use techniques, but the support and co-operation of those around her enhance the chance of her success. In our minds, the following community attitudes and resources are important to rape prevention.

All women must feel that they are not alone, that resources concerning sexual assault are available to them. A rape-crisis center in the region is a necessity. Other supportive resources might be rap groups, block watches, crime-prevention programs *and* a police department that will believe her if she reports the incident.

Women must also be able to recognize potentially dangerous situations. An important component is responsible, informative media. Not only does the media generally need to present rape in a more realistic way, it also needs to inform the public, in a non-sensational manner, of specific situations that warrant caution. Constructive alternatives or responses should be presented through the media. In order to utilize such knowledge, a woman needs to have a healthy skepticism. To feel good about her own intuition and reactions, she needs the support and validation of those around her. She should not be judged silly or paranoid for acting to protect herself.

It is important that each woman have her own safety—not the good will of the man harassing her—as her first priority. The process of internalizing our priorities is basically done alone through self-concept exercises, examining how we feel about other women and ourselves, and actually beginning to express our rights. Conversations with other women in the same process, practicing self-concept exercises with other people and acceptance of a new assertive attitude by those closest to us are very important.

Knowledge of our bodies, feelings of integration between spirit and body and the certainty that our bodies will defend us are all crucial to rape prevention. Self-defense practice and physical exertion are important in testing our durability and in expanding our physical limits. Community resources to this end can start in the elementary schools with equal participation in all sports for boys and girls. For those of us who lacked this valuable school experience, an array of classes for adult women to expand their physical skills is needed. Team sports are particularly special for teaching that winning is a reality and in building support among women.

Finally, when the individual woman finds herself in a situation that she does not want to be in, she needs to have an idea of what she will do next and be able to follow through on that. This incorporates all of the previous elements of rape prevention. Practicing "What-if Games" can be the means to the end of a definite, self-protective response to a potentially dangerous situation. On a larger scale, the combination of self-preservation, accurate constructive information, supportive resources and individual skill development should become an inherent part of our daily functioning.

At this point, we would like you to return to the three cases in the first chapter. Have your attitudes or reactions changed? It is important to know how those changes specifically affect you. We hope that this book has given you a better understanding of rape and increased your options for responding. We also hope you've discovered things you already do well but had not previously recognized.

When some, and hopefully all of the elements we listed above become reality, we can, as a culture, in Susan Brownmiller's words "deny rape its future." As individual women, we can change our reflex of fear into a reflex of action.

APPENDIX

USING THIS BOOK
WITH GROUPS

Adolescents

by Claudia Black, M.S.W.

Claudia Black is a social worker with the Rape Prevention Forum. She has also been a social worker in residential treatment facilities for adolescent women. Her areas of specialized training are psychodrama and assertiveness training.

As adolescent girls are struggling to find their autonomy, sexual identity is the paramount issue. As they are responding to menstruation, growing breasts, new body hairs, they are much more atune to sexual statements. Adolescence is a time when the young person is questioning, challenging parental opinions and messages she has heard and lived by her entire life. Peers become more important than they have ever been. What others think of them, particularly peers, is of major importance. The teen-ager is making new decisions for herself. She is experiencing a new form of strength within herself, and testing new behaviors. This leads to great amounts of anxiety, confusion and self-doubt, leaving the adolescent very vulnerable. The influence of the movies and the media affects the teen-age girl in a manner that perpetuates her vulnerability.

In adolescence, when one is curious about sex and relationships with members of the opposite sex, the media helps the young woman learn well it is her role to negate her feelings if someone wants her attention. To be overcome sexually is portrayed as glamorous. We see a very beautiful woman in a movie, on television, arguing with a man. As the argument ensues, the woman becomes angrier. The man wavers between anger and amusement. The woman decides to make a dramatic exit. She moves toward the door. The man reaches out, grabs her, pulls her to him. He kisses her. She gives in with a passionate embrace. Message: All she really wanted was for him to kiss her. She can forget all other concerns because he is, in fact, interested in her physically.

Another strong message given to the young woman is that if a man wants to kiss you, relax. We see scene after scene where a woman begins to struggle and once she gives in she, in fact, enjoys it. Never is the message: If you don't want it to happen, say so, and be firm.

Very few adolescents have developed a very solid, positive self-concept. There is confusion and/or ambivalence about who they are, what they want. There is often a lack of information or knowledge about possible consequences of sexual behavior. The theme portrayed most consistently via movies and television that relates to sexual encounters is that when single men and women meet, they will like each other. They will be attracted to each other. The man will initiate the contact, while the woman has longed for the contact. The man and woman will kiss and then trail off happily. Seldom do we get messages that men and women can be friends without a sexual interest, that a woman can initiate contacts with members of the opposite sex. Nor do we get the message that women can do many other things in life than fantasize about present or future romantic relationships.

Typically, only the most beautiful women are portrayed with men on television. Where is the role for the less physically attractive and articulate woman? Many adolescents wonder if they are able or even deserve to have relationships with men. While the so-called less "attractive" woman wonders if she can have relationships with men, the more "beautiful" woman learns well what her *one* role is to be.

The authors discuss the dilemma presented because media so often portrays rape as the stranger-to-stranger surprise attack. When a woman is forced into intercourse with someone she knows, she feels confused and may even doubt she was raped. This dilemma is a double jeopardy for the teen-ager who is not yet clear on territorial issues, is not yet sure who is responsible for what behavior. Many young women fall prey to the myth: Allow a man to be sexually active with you and he will not be able to control himself. The message the woman receives is that she is then responsible for his behavior.

As the adolescent woman becomes sexually active, she begins with some body touching, hand holding, kissing, fondling, possibly oral sex. For a young person who does not want to have intercourse but has entered into other sexual behavior, she most often will hear an ultimatum. You owe it to me. You can't expect me to go this far without the rest. I'll go find another girl who will do it. Young women often enter into intercourse responding to an ultimatum and/or feeling they are responsible for this man's sexual state and they owe it to him. This is a social rape, a real rape, and one you will not see portrayed by the media.

The rape against the adolescent woman most often portrayed is via the film media when a young woman is hitchhiking. The underlying message is that she is responsible because she was hitchhiking. She puts herself in a vulnerable position when she hitchhikes, but she is not asking to be raped. She still wants to pick and choose who she is sexually active with. Another part of the dilemma in this portrayal is that it implies that most adolescent rape takes place in cars while hitchhiking. It again implies the stranger-to-stranger dynamic. Neither of which is true.

Recently, in speaking with a sixteen-year-old, she told me of her sense of guilt and feelings of responsibility for being raped while on a date. En route to a movie, the date announced to the girl that he wanted to stop by a friend's house before going to the movie. The young woman said she did not want to, but said she would have felt "stupid" saying she didn't want to go to the friend's house. Therefore she said nothing. When they arrived at the friend's house, the young woman did not want to go in. Again fearful she would sound stupid if she said how she felt, she went in. She said she didn't want her date to think she didn't trust him. Upon entering the house, the girl was surrounded by eight men and raped. The girl said she was too frightened to do anything.

This teen-ager has not yet told her parents, feeling ashamed, humiliated and responsible. After all, she saw three opportunities for possible defense prior to the rape. (1) She could have said assertively that she did not want to stop at the friend's house, but wanted to go directly to the movie. (2) She could have waited in the car for her date while he visited. (3) She could have tried fleeing when she was outnumbered. In looking at proper etiquette, this young woman responded very politely. One of the dynamics implicit in this situation is the power implied related to etiquette rule Number Six: "It Is the Natural State of Affairs for Men to Carry the Financial Burden of Social Situations." When a man carries this role of providing the money for entertainment, he is often given the power for decision making. We have learned that that prerogative gives him the power for greater decision making. Another unspoken rule is: If you cannot give an explanation for what you want, then it's not justifiable.

This young woman knew she did not want to go in, but felt that in itself was not enough justification for her to feel confident enough to say what she wanted. Another dynamic in this rape relates to rule Number Three: "We Must Not Bother Other People or Make a Scene Because We Are Uncomfortable." This young woman said she did not run for fear of making a scene.

As stated earlier and demonstrated in the above experience, adolescents are often very confused about territoriality—who has what rights. They are experiencing a lot of doubt when it comes to trusting themselves, particularly when it is relative to those in more powerful positions. Adolescent boys are in those powerful positions (ascribed power). Boys or men often carry the financial burden, are physically larger, and are the ones girls or women are to focus their lives upon.

I would like to add another rule adolescents often ascribe to: "It Is Not Fair to Others to Change Your Mind Once You Have Stated Something." One example of this rule is when a young woman agrees to go to a party with a young man; while at the party, she decides she does not like this person; she doesn't trust him. She feels she will be safer if he does not take her home. She has the right to change her mind about the plans originally agreed on for the evening. Another example, a young woman has sex with her boy friend one night. She can change her mind and decide not to be sexually active with him the next night. Feelings change. That is human.

I would like to recommend to those professionals working with adolescents to take each etiquette rule described in this text and, one at a time, view the rule so that you can see how conforming to the rule was at one's personal expense. Rape will not be the result of all situations. It may not be the result of any for these particular adolescents. But they will be able to find a sense of emotional violation. I believe all young women will be able to identify with the etiquette rules, and viewing the rules in this manner will assist in clarifying values and building self-concepts as they learn about themselves and are able to understand previously confusing dynamics.

Being liked, being noticed, is very important to most people. It is particularly important to adolescents. Often, teen-agers are identifying who they are as a result of their interactions with others. When they are subscribing to a book of etiquette rules that often lead to their own violation, with no clarity of their rights and priorities, they are inevitable victims.

I very much agree with the concept that how you feel about yourself is directly related to your ability to defend yourself. Because of the tumultuous nature of adolescent years, it is particularly important that we do what we can to enhance self-esteem to assist in making the adolescent less vulnerable sexually.

The idea that one is being selfish and/or conceited for thinking positively of oneself is nearly a law of adolescent girls. As much as we all need compliments, for the adolescent female, there is an even greater need *not* to appear conceited. It is particularly difficult for them to say positive things about themselves. For the more esteemed young woman, it may be possible to say positive things about herself, but with embarrassment. Ask an adolescent to listen to a positive statement made about them, they'll invariably respond with "Yes, but . . ." Young women need permission to feel good about themselves and to stroke themselves for what is true. That is realism, not conceit. Conceit enters when we use our positive attributes to hurt or manipulate others. It is all right to acknowledge positive attributes about oneself. Liking oneself is a wonderful experience. It leads to our confidence in our abilities to handle situations, often the unknown. We are less likely to be intimidated by others. We are more likely to respond in a manner that will defend ourselves when necessary.

It is important to view catastrophes in the sense that adolescents do to understand further their dilemma in getting out of vulnerable situations. Adolescents often feel that to stay in a situation they distrust will be less of a catastrophe than to draw attention to themselves. Realizing the need to be "cool," it is an even greater risk to draw attention to themselves if they think there is a chance that others will think they don't deserve it or are being stupid. Adolescents don't have that self-trust in judging situations. They don't have that trust that others will perceive the situation as they do. As a twelve-year-old, I remember being at a junior high dance that took place outdoors in a park. The sixty-five-year-old park caretaker walked over and asked me to dance. I didn't want to, but did so out of politeness. This man held me very close and wouldn't let go of me after the dance. I was scared, knew I wanted to get away, but felt that if I told the chaperones there might be a scene. I wasn't sure I had the right to feel that way because the chaperones didn't act in a manner that showed they thought anything was wrong. For me, in this case, and for many young people, the catastrophe cannot be clearly defined, but the sense of catastrophe is all about us. To be embarrassed and to not be trusted are two of the greater catastrophes in adolescence.

In noting that "Critical Tapes" affects our self-esteem, I would like to point out that adolescents are probably the most self-critical age group of people. They are experiencing a change in physical identity and a change in values and in power. Little is stable for this age group. There is a lot of insecurity in their new world, a dynamic critical tapes plays on. For this reason, I would strongly encourage the use of "First Thoughts" with this age group. The practice of Exercises 2–5 will also greatly enhance the adolescent woman's self-image as she identifies with her own power, rather than feeling intimidated in relating to others.

In "What-if Games," the authors suggest adding one's own situations to the list. I would like to add a few situations that specifically focus ·on the younger woman:

"What if you are home alone? Dad's friend comes over to the house to borrow some tools. You feel this visit is odd because this man knows no one is home but you, and he was here just a few hours ago when your parents were here."

"What if you have been going out with a guy four months? You have kissed, fondled. He now says he has waited long enough. He loves you. But he has to have more."

"What if you are at a party and after you have been sexually active with a boy, he leaves the room and another boy comes in and begins to take his clothes off?"

In closing the section on adolescents, I would like to heartily support the use of physical self-defense as presented in this book. The adolescent person is experiencing tremendous body changes. With those changes are conflicting feelings of joy, embarrassment, delight, shame, disgust, awe, etc. Viewing our body as is emphasized in *In Defense of Ourselves* enables us to appreciate our body as a friend. Women can come to realize the potential of their bodies if given such messages. The *earlier* a woman can feel the ability not to be overcome physically by a man, the less traumatic one's adolescent years can be. Adolescence is a fearful time. It is a time of sexual exploration. We can take a great amount of fear out of the adolescent process by practicing the concepts discussed in reference to physical self-defense.

The Older Woman

by Esther Myerding

Esther Myerding is a mother of four children. Her work experience has been in the field of education, and she presently works with the American Friends Service Committee in Seattle, Washington.

Older women are no more like each other than younger women are like each other. Our personal histories, interacting with our race, class and other societal factors, produce individuals with widely differing attitudes, abilities, and limitations. After reading *In Defense of Ourselves,* however, I think there are some special considerations for older women in the area of rape prevention. Our biggest asset as older women—our many years of experience—can become our biggest liability when we are faced with the threat of rape. Too often, these years of experience have also been years when we were "conditioned" to be victims: when information on rape and rape prevention was scarce and inaccurate, when our self-concepts as women and as physically competent people were weakened, and when restrictive rules of etiquette became ingrained in our minds.

Perhaps one of the greatest differences for older women is the atmosphere that surrounded our early education about rape. I can't remember ever knowing anyone who told me she had been a rape victim. Undoubtedly there were women I had much contact with who had been raped, but I never knew of it first-hand, and no doubt very few other people in their lives did either. This is very different now. Probably many of us, of any age, know at least one woman who has been a rape victim. Young women learn about rape and its prevention from increasingly abundant literature, media coverage and even classes. An important result of this change is that most young rape victims are better equipped to deal with rape and its effects than are older victims, many of whom are still just learning to think and talk about rape in an open, practical, self-affirming way.

I'm not sure that the chances of being raped have increased over the years, but my perception of that likelihood has changed. Because the social values and rules were so different in my youth, my understanding of the realities of rape has had to change also. Many older women, like me, grew up in close-knit families where our activities as children were supervised most of the time and where we developed deep feelings of security. The idea of sexual violence within the family was unheard of—and unthinkable; we thought of rapists as being only strangers. As a result, we as older women carry with us many of the traditional myths about who rapists are. It is true, of course, that many younger women share these myths, but older women have been living with these misconceptions longer and generally have been less exposed to education about the reality behind the myths. Most rape-information sources seem aimed at younger women, perhaps because we are all "conditioned" to think that (1) rape is a sexual crime, (2) older women are non-sexual, and therefore, (3) older women do not get raped. The false stereotype of older women as sexless reinforces the shame and isolation felt by many older rape victims. For many older women, it may be especially difficult to consider the non-stranger (family member, neighbor, service personnel, etc.) as potentially dangerous.

The commercial media have become increasingly important as attitude-molders during the life-span of my generation, and the media provide older women with many damaging images of ourselves. When we are not fumbling and helpless old women, we are rigid and fascistic mothers or mothers-in-law. We are rarely shown being supportive of each other or of our daughters. More often we are portrayed as being competitive and difficult to live with. Comparison of older women's media image with older men's media image is even more telling. Both older men and older women may be presented as experts or voices of authority in TV commercials, for example. However, the man knows about banks, investments, real estate, insurance and cars, while the woman knows about making coffee, cleaning sinks, and the right thickness of soup. The man shares his wisdom with logic and charm; the woman informs through ridicule and aggressiveness. The acceptable physical attributes are different as well. Gray hair is "distinguished" in men but makes a woman look older than her husband, which of course she must never be. The scuffling or stumbling gait ascribed to older women is mocked by comedians more often than that ascribed to older men.

This kind of negative media image reinforces older women's "conditioning" as victims and may have significant effect on an older woman's ability (or inability) to prepare herself against rape. Moreover, the fact that younger women, as well as older women, often unconsciously absorb this media image of older women keeps women of different ages from being mutually supportive. An older woman who has been thoughtlessly "put down" by younger women because of her age— or because of age-related differences like clothes, hairstyle, hobbies, etc.—will not turn to younger women for support when she is a victim of rape.

One major difference in the media for older women lies in the romantic movie. According to *In Defense of Ourselves*, women's self-concepts have been affected negatively by comparisons with unrealistic "romantic" relationships in the media. I do not find this to be true for myself. Although we did not have TV in my "formative years," we did have some of the most unrealistic, fantasy-oriented movies that have ever been made. These movies were the mainstay of our entertainment. What is different for older women, I think, is that we recognized those plots as unreal and did not try to measure our own lives by these portrayals of "happiness." Perhaps younger women today do not easily discern the difference between media fantasy and everyday reality.

Almost all of the etiquette rules are firm and binding in many older women's minds. These rules go beyond mere "politeness" and handicap us with a complete, subconscious set of expectations—for our own behavior and that of other people. There are things I have never done simply because the rules of etiquette with which I grew up decreed they were inappropriate for a young woman—or for any "nice" woman. In a case of threatened rape, some of these "inappropriate" behaviors might be life savers. Again, most women have been subjected to some etiquette training, but we older women have had more years for these rules to become ingrained.

For many older women, the crux of this book could be the self-concept chapter. Our own long-standing poor self-concepts can be our greatest liability. Although older women outnumber men, many of us believe that men are absolutely necessary for some important tasks: handling of money, repairs around the house, etc. Some women believe men are inherently suited for these tasks. Also, many older women might not trust other women with personal information because they have a strong sense of privacy, and unfortunately, they perceive men as protecting those rights. Not only do men sometimes not protect those rights, but the woman's appraisal of other women is a reflection of her own poor self-concept.

I believe the older woman's sense of self can be more complicated than a younger woman's. One of the more obvious reasons is that self-concept can become a habit—one that she has had for sixty years or more. Another reason is that older women have been longer under the expectations of others. As children, we lived under the expectations of our parents. Many of us married young and immediately took on the expectations of our husbands. Those of us who had children then began living up to our children's expectations of what mothers are. This pattern is changing for some young women as they choose to deal only with their own expectations for themselves.

Another indication of low self-esteem is that many older women have a special problem with accepting compliments. It seems we rarely talk about ourselves. We may seek compliments about our grandchildren, our husbands' accomplishments, our homes, etc., but some of us would never take seriously a compliment about our own accomplishments. Even those of us who feel we do have something to offer the world and are living independently may be uncomfortable with compliments. All of us have been taught that accepting a compliment as an accurate reflection of our own self-worth is being conceited and immodest.

On the positive side, I believe that older women suffer less from "catastrophic expectations." We have survived so many events that are gravely anticipated. Every time we successfully come through a difficult situation, we learn that we do have the capacity to cope (mastery over our environment) and that we will survive in the future. Such episodes reaffirm our faith in life and in ourselves. As we accumulate more good relationships and experiences, we may be able to let go of less-desirable relationships or experiences more easily than younger people can.

In the area of physical self-defense, I think the older woman is more limited. As we age, we become more aware of our physical limitations. This is all in the natural process of aging. We should not be ashamed of it, yet we often participate in "Black Cloudisms" and conclude that we are no longer worthwhile or capable. This process is bound to affect the older woman's appraisal of her ability to physically defend herself.

I also feel that few older women would trust themselves to use these techniques, and in fact, could not envision themselves successfully executing the techniques at any age, due both to strong etiquette conditioning and to a self-concept that dictates lack of physical skill. For older women who do consider physical defense as an option, I feel it is vitally important to heed the words of caution in this book. If we intend to use the techniques, we must be willing to incapacitate the assailant. We must be quick, confident and highly skilled through practice.

The life experience of older women puts us in a good position to cope with some forms of sexual violence. Some of us have overcome our conditioning to be "ladies." The Depression and World War II spurred many women (who are now older women) to set aside that conditioning and do what we had to do in order to survive. After the war was over, many of us forgot those strong, capable selves and returned to the habits of our original training. Why not use some of these experiences in the self-concept exercises?

Older women may be free in some sense for the first time in their lives. Their authority figures (parents, husbands or even children) may be gone or uninvolved. They no longer need to justify their existence with a job—in or out of their homes. If they have the financial resources, they can absorb themselves in their own interests. It is the time to embrace the thesis of *In Defense of Ourselves*—to like ourselves, to like each other—to continue to survive successfully.

Aging in America is often an unpleasant reality. I do not mean to imply that the older woman faced with a potentially violent situation needs only to draw on her inner resources. Yet, a first step to curb our victimization is to instill a confident attitude in ourselves. We have infinite resources within ourselves to do this.

Rural Women

by Sharon Ryals

Sharon Ryals is a volunteer who helped set up Thurston County Rape Relief and Reduction, Olympia, Washington. In writing this section, she drew on her experiences of living and working in rural Washington, discussions with women working in the field of rural social work (Sharon Brogan and Susan Russell), and with women who grew up in rural environments. She does not, however, consider herself an "expert" on rural women, and does not attempt to speak for all rural women.

I want to say a few words first about Thurston County Rape Relief and Reduction. This group serves a tri-city area of about 40,000 people; the remainder of the county is largely rural. Of the twenty calls coming in to us during 1977 from women who had been raped or assaulted, twelve of the assaults took place in a rural area.

A rural woman may have some misconceptions about rape. She might consider the crime as one that happens in the big, bad city, to women who are on the street at night and who are attacked by hideous strangers.

Because there are·fewer strangers in the country, we think it is safer. We are not prepared to deal with the man down the road, our brother's friends, our friend's father, someone we are dating, or an ex boy friend.

But rape does happen in rural areas, to all kinds of women who are living their normal daily lives. Later I will mention some "what if" situations that rural women have found themselves in.

Just as in the rest of our culture, women who grow up in rural areas learn what is expected of them as women. One of the strongest role models for rural women is the farm wife or earth mother. She is a strong woman who feeds and cares for a large family and the hired help, tends the garden and animals, cans, makes clothing and does an incredible amount of work singlehandedly. She is strong, nurturing and relies on her own abilities. She also is completely self-sacrificing, never thinks of her own needs and is highly isolated. In spite of her strength and skills, however, she must never best a man in any situation. She is taught to feel helpless to defend herself and to turn to men for their greater wisdom and protection. The role of farm wife/earth mother is not really an option that many rural women have, but it is often the ideal that they look up to.

Another role for women is prescribed by country Western music, which almost invariably portrays women as helpless, submissive and victimized. This woman's identity comes from her man, and she will always be loyal to him no matter how many times he runs out on her, drinks up the paycheck or knocks her around the house. The counterpart of this role is one for men that shows them as hard-working, independent, violent, domineering, wild and possibly needing to be "tamed" by a good woman, although not to any great degree.

Some of the teachings of American etiquette that particularly apply to rural women are that we must always be open, friendly and helpful to neighbors and strangers. The friendliness of country people is a reason many people choose to live in rural areas. It becomes very hard for us to ignore or refuse help to someone because the person or the situation makes us uncomfortable.

What if a stranger comes to the door saying his car has broken down? You are alone and the nearest house with other people at home is several miles away. What do you do? Most of the time we are safe to respond as helpfully as we can without fear of being in danger. But we do need to pay attention to what we feel and be willing to respond directly and assertively if the person becomes offensive or threatening. If you choose not to let someone in, you might hurt his feelings, but your safety is much more important.

The notion that a man always pays is prevalent in rural areas. There are few jobs available to rural women. Few rural women have much money, and even fewer can afford to live economically independent of parents or husband. Under most circumstances it makes sense for a man to pay. However, this does not give him the right to demand sexual payment in return.

Because there are so few opportunities for women in rural areas other than marriage and economic dependence, many women leave as soon as they get out of high school. They go to college or to the city where there are jobs. In rural areas men outnumber women two to one.

Many rural women become highly isolated in their homes. They are especially isolated from other women. Because economic survival for women is so dependent on their marrying a good man, sometimes mistrust and competition between women is intensified. With fewer women around many women grow up with no female friends and have to establish themselves in a largely male-defined society.

The methods we are taught to use to deal with harassment tend to reinforce both the idea that we can't really do anything for ourselves and that we are at fault when someone attacks us. One woman told me that when she complained to her mother about her brother's friends who had threatened her, her mother told her to stay away from them and everything would be just fine. One day she was out gathering eggs and the boys came by and saw her in the chicken coop alone. She felt that it was her fault that she had been cornered, and she should have known better than to go out and gather eggs that morning.

The method of always looking to men for protection also has its limitations. Often another man is not available to call on. I myself began to be very careful about asking men for protection when I saw how easy it was for many men to use "protecting the lady's honor" as an excuse for beating the daylights out of another man. Competition among men for female attention is also very intense in rural areas, and many times I have seen men brutalize each other in the name of "protecting their women." And then the woman is generally blamed for starting the fight.

In spite of the expectation that we must turn to men for protection, many rural women are constantly facing challenges alone with only their own good intelligence, strength and skill to rely on. Acknowledging and reminding ourselves of why we deserve to be here tomorrow, what we like about ourselves, and examining our very real strengths are particularly useful to rural women.

The isolation of many women has been one of the main reasons for a long tradition of durable, self-reliant rural women. We developed our survival skills because we had to, but it is often a lonely experience. Isolation and lack of support from other women were two of the main things that a group of rural women in Lincoln County felt were the greatest difficulties rural women face. A women's group was started and was advertised carefully so that women who were suspicious of the women's liberation movement would still feel comfortable about coming. For most of the women in the group it was a rare opportunity to get together with other women. Many felt that they were able to express feelings about their lives that they never before expressed. They chose to do some assertiveness training work, and through each other's support many developed a really positive love for themselves. Using the exercises described in this book would be particularly useful in that kind of situation.

Given some of the problems rural women face, the misinformation about rape we receive, and both the strengths and hindrances of our highly stressed feminine roles, I want to list some realistic potential rape situations rural women have encountered.

You are thirteen and are out gathering eggs. Two of your brother's friends walk by and see you there alone. They begin to tease you and make sexually threatening remarks.

You are walking to the mailbox, a mile and a half down the road. A stranger drives by and asks for directions. He drives on, then turns around and comes back by you two more times. He stops on the road ahead of you and gets out of his car and starts walking toward you.

You are hitchhiking into town and a neighbor picks you up. He turns off the main road and starts fondling you, saying he knows you've always been interested in him.

You are driving into town and pick up the son of a neighbor. He suggests you skip going to town and take care of a "thing" you have going.

You are home alone in the middle of the day. Your husband and everyone else are out on a logging show. A man whose car has broken down comes to the door and wants to come in. There is no other house to send him to.

You are on a date and go for a drive. At some point your date insists that you either put out or get out. You are several miles from the nearest house on an infrequently traveled road.

You come home one day and find your husband's friend drunk on your couch. (Of course the door wasn't locked, and he's a friend.) He makes insulting remarks and doesn't plan on leaving.

Many young women who live in rural areas hitchhike or catch rides with neighbors because they do not own or have access to a car, and there is no public transportation. Self-defense in a car is sometimes difficult, but not impossible, particularly if you know that just because he's given you a ride, he doesn't have the right to demand sexual payment for it, and that you didn't ask for his abuse because you asked for transportation. One woman called us to report an incident in which she had gotten a ride from a man outside a small town. On a rural highway several miles out of town he stopped and got out, saying he had to check a tire. Then he got back in and reached over and grabbed her. She smashed him in the nose with the heel of her hand, jumped out of the car and ran into the dense brush and woods by the side of the road. After he drove off, she came out and flagged down another car.

If hitchhiking is a necessity for you, listen to your own intuition. If something about the situation bothers you, don't get in the car or else demand to be let out immediately. Practice using the elbow-to-the-nose strike described on page 76. Practice it with a friend sitting in a car. Practice getting out of a car fast.

This book can be useful in a women's group. Particularly important for rural women are the exercises concerning acknowledging what we like about ourselves, assessing our strengths and imagining using our abilities to defend ourselves. Although the book can be useful to one woman by herself, it would be more useful to do the verbal and physical exercises with one or more other women. Hopefully, it will stimulate rural women to reach out to one another.

Lesbians

by Kathleen Boyle

Kathleen Boyle is Co-director of the Lesbian Women's Resource Center at the University YWCA in Seattle, Washington. She has been counseling Lesbians through the Center for the past three years.

There is no reliable estimate of how many rape victims are Lesbians; but Lesbians *do* get raped. However, it is difficult to state conclusions about the nature and extent of all rapes involving Lesbians, mainly because Lesbians are not readily distinguishable.

They represent all ethnic groups, all economic classes, all sizes, shapes and appearances. Like other women, they attend school, hold a variety of jobs ranging from cook to carpenter, missionary to scientist, go to the movies and the beach, climb mountains and buy new shoes. Some Lesbians live alone, some live with other women, still others struggle to support their children. They differ from their sisters only in their sexual orientation.

Another equally significant reason for lack of data in this area is the general assumption that all women are heterosexual. The good-looking forty-five-year-old mother of two reporting a rape is assumed to be heterosexual because she doesn't fit the stereotyped image of a sexual minority woman. Because of common attitudes and responses to Lesbianism, this woman probably won't risk revealing her sexual preference when she is already in a vulnerable situation—that of a rape victim. She knows that her identity as a Lesbian might cause her to be rejected ("You deserved to be raped!") or to receive inadequate care and protection ("We can't bother with the likes of you").

She also knows the popular myth that someway she, the victim, provoked the rape and that her Lesbianism could easily be used as proof that she antagonizes men. If she wishes to bring her rapist to justice, she must continue to let everyone think she is heterosexual. Her familiarity with rape trials will tell her that the victim's moral conduct is often used to discredit her and to exonerate the rapist. Since Lesbianism is still considered immoral behavior by many, she knows that her rapist might avoid prosecution if her sexual preference is known.

However, even without statistics, there are some general conclusions we can draw about Lesbians and rape.

1. Lesbians are not exempt from rape situations. The fact that a woman does not live with a man or does not date men does not remove her from all dangerous

situations. The fact is that most rapes are planned and that Lesbians avoid only those rapes that grow out of a dating situation.

2. Lesbians find themselves in many of the same circumstances as other rape victims. There are few places or activities in society that are not a part of the lives of all women, including Lesbians. Lesbians drive cars, go to shopping centers, wait for buses, answer the doorbell, walk their dogs, hitchhike, jog in the morning and drive their children to school. Each of these activities is a potential setting for a rapist. Of concern is the fact that Lesbians are more likely to do these things alone than are other women. Many Lesbians manage to be autonomous and do not, for example, look for escorts when going on a walk or doing their daily jog.

It would also seem that a house that does not contain a man might look like a good target to a rapist. In the case of planned rape, the rapist might pick homes where a woman is alone or those at which he expects little resistance. Thus, it would seem that one or two women living in a household would be more vulnerable in an environment less obvious than the street.

Furthermore, Lesbians often go to social spots also frequented by heterosexual women and men. Since many people assume that a woman without a male escort is looking for one, men sometimes harass such women because they believe the women welcome it.

Because the Lesbian does not necessarily look any different than her heterosexual or bisexual sisters, the potential rapist may assume that she's the perfect victim. She's going to be helpless, and she's going to like it. Certainly the myth that all women want to be raped doesn't apply to her any more than to any other woman, but the rapist doesn't know that. He sees her only as another potential victim.

3. Lesbians are more likely to be raped by strangers than by men who are known to them. Since most Lesbians are not involved in dating situations with men, they are not very likely to be forced into "paying" for dates. Since they are not involved in emotionally loaded dating situations with men, they often have comfortable friendships with men who are not concerned about them as sexual objects. There are also Lesbians whose lives do not include men at all. For all of these women the threat with which they are most often faced is of an encounter with a stranger.

4. Some rapists pick women whom they know are Lesbians in order to "teach them a lesson." Occasionally an individual man will plan a revenge rape against a woman who he thinks has thwarted his desire for a relationship with her. If he has been rejected by a woman he knows is a Lesbian, he may be affronted by her life-style and feel that he must defend his honor as a male by raping her.

Some women in this situation have reported that the rapist has told them that all they really needed was a good lay to "straighten" them out. There have also been a few reported cases of gang rapes in which a group of males, reacting to a woman as a Lesbian, have decided to "punish" her for stepping outside the boundaries they think are appropriate for women.

In this case, the rape usually follows some incident in which the men in question felt they had obtained "proof" of the victim's Lesbianism; for example, two women seen together in a restaurant or a woman dressing in a manner that they see as "like a man." That not all women raped in this circumstance are Lesbians is an important fact. It is the perception of the rapist that women *should* be accompanied by a man and *should* be punished for behaving in ways he doesn't find appropriate.

The self-concept and assertiveness sections of this book are as important to Lesbian readers as the self-defense section. Because of the negative value attached to her life-style by many members of this society, the average Lesbian may not have a very healthy self-concept. Along with the poor image she may have internalized about herself as a woman, she has the added burden of being devalued by society because she is not defined by a relationship with a man.

If she is unable to be open about her life-style (because she fears losing a job, children, housing or friends), she may have a difficult time feeling like a valuable human being. Perhaps she doesn't feel good about her life-style as well, due to lack of education or lack of support in her circle. In addition to improving her self-esteem, the Lesbian reader who is uncomfortable about the cultural judgment of her life-style might be well-advised to contact the homophile organization nearest her for information and support. These organizations can help her deal with cultural pressures as well as the myths and stereotypes she herself may hold about her situation.

Both the "American Etiquette" and "Seven Exercises" sections are extremely helpful for Lesbians who need to improve their skills in interactions with men who are annoying them. There are, of course, a great many Lesbians who handle themselves clearly and assertively, but unfortunately many women, Lesbians or not, fall into two other categories of behavior: timid and elusive, or hostile and abusive.

The timid and elusive woman tends to behave as she perceives men wish her to behave. She wishes to avoid confrontation and tries not to hurt someone's feelings by telling him to go away or that she is being annoyed by him. If she is a Lesbian wishing to remain inconspicuous, she may be afraid that her rejection will be a signal to him that she is a Lesbian. She's afraid that he'll say, "What's wrong with you, are you a lezzie?" Consequently, she may become elusive, apologetic, unclear. This behavior will only strike the offender as a sign that she is vulnerable. He may even take her confusion as shyness and a cue that she really wants him to continue his approach.

On the other hand, some women, many of them Lesbians, are hostile and verbally abusive to men who approach them, and sometimes this behavior provokes an attack. There is a distinct difference between assertive behavior and abusive behavior. To some women, every man is a potential rapist, and their anger about this becomes their own worst enemy. It is worth noting that abusive behavior provokes anger and often violence. The offender who might have been content just to harass a woman might feel the need to "punish" her if she attacks him or puts him down cruelly. This could lead her to be the victim of a planned rape later on. Without a doubt, it is important—indeed vital—for women to be assertive in order to preserve their rights, but abusive behavior is apt to be a signal for more dangerously abusive behavior in return.

That Lesbians are in need of the physical self-defense techniques in this book is very clear. As women who have chosen not to spend their lives under the "protection" of men, they run a great risk of being caught in situations where their only source of defense is themselves.

It would be desirable for women reading this book to share its contents with their friends. Perhaps Lesbian groups or organizations could arrange workshops to test out the skills described here and to arrange practice sessions for their members. Certainly concerned Lesbians would be wise to arrange "buddy systems"; someone with whom to practice, someone to monitor their assertiveness skills.

It is also advisable to check out personal habits. Am I often alone? Do I live alone? Do I park my bike in the shadows? Is it late at night when I get off work? These and many other circumstances should be checked by group members.

After all, women working together is the only way that we will no longer be victims.

The Black Woman

by Allethia Allen, M.S.W.

Allethia Allen is an assistant professor in the School of Social Work, University of Washington, Seattle. She teaches Social Work Practice, Human Sexuality and has had extensive practice and administrative experience in the Social Work Community.

The subject of rape prevention as discussed *In Defense of Ourselves* presents a realistic approach for *all* women. The basic philosophy and instruction of adequate physical defense, psychological and emotional influences and assertive efforts to prevent a forced sexual contact are imperative. The quick perception of the rapist's intentions, coupled with the discussion of a woman's determination and *right* to survive definitely influence her positive-coping techniques in a dangerous situation. Whatever the racial background of a woman, she is a part of a society that has not completely prepared her for the total disregard of her rights and defense of her total self. This book is important in the instruction of women for the prevention of one of the most negative of experiences. In a matter of fact way it has a positive message about a healthy approach to everyday life.

The subject of rape and the black woman presents some interesting contrasts and conflicts since the cause of rape in some instance is directly related to the denial, deprivation and poor economic and social conditions created for black people. For the most part, many black women and men find themselves in a disadvantaged position in American society, continually coping with efforts to survive and to progress. The social role and conflicts of black people, sexual myths about blacks and economic and social oppression all contribute to the adjustment of the potential rapist and to the position of the woman who is a potential victim. The position of whites and others in a white-dominated society also has influence on the problem of rape and permission or restrictions that the potential rapist and victim allow themselves. All are interwoven in this drama of violence in American life.

There is a special significance to the matter of black-white relations in this country which directly relates to the taboos and permitted sexual behavior for black or white men and women in general. With the history of slavery, the ensuing political and social oppression, social and economic deprivation, the role of black people may be perceived by the white majority culture as being an inferior way of life with special emphasis on the inferior status of men and women in a non-white culture. Frequently, it has not mattered that separate from the majority culture there has been the development of a fantastically rich black culture which in many instances supersede contributions of the white culture. Often the contributions are measured according to white standards, customs and procedures without the overlay of history or positive perceptions of current adaptive adjustments. Often then, sexual contact across racial lines has not been an accepted mode of behavior and has provided an opportunity for forced participation or rape by those who see this as a means of imposing will on a disadvantaged group.

In Gerda Lerner's book *Black Women in White America**, there is much discussion of the rape of black women as a weapon of terror. This follows the course of history and is discussed as a technique used in oppression. She states:

> The practice of raping the women of a defeated enemy is world-wide and is found in every culture. The occurrence of this practice during many race riots and during periods of terror against blacks at various times in U.S. history merely affirms the colonial nature of the oppression of black people in the U.S. It is the ultimate expression of contempt for a defeated foe since it symbolizes *his* helplessness more fully than any other conceivable act.

Often the historical records do not lend interpretations of isolated acts of criminal individuals, who in addition to the political climate add to the oppressive nature of forcible rape of black women in a system of racial and economic exploitation. This doubly adds to the problems.

In our modern world, since the advent of civil rights, blacks are still struggling against the perception of being a conquered people. They have always designed adaptive maneuvers to survive and to preserve a social system which has prescribed rules for social behavior based on an original culture of their own from Africa. This, combined primarily with the Judeo-Christian system, has provided many innovations in their way of life regarding sex and accepted behavior.

> Black sexuality has always held a certain mystique for white Americans, and one can only wonder why, since both the positive and negative aspects of black sexual behavior are results of white racism. A look at history demonstrates that the sexual behavior of Black Africans was strictly regulated by the customs of the different African societies until their brutal transplantation to the new world. Unlike the Victorian code of sexual behavior so endemic to whites, Africans saw sex as a matter between individuals and not determined by God.

The women of Africa were brought to this country to service the lust of the white master class. Although black women had other functions in the domestic and labor realm, their major task was to bear the brunt of the double standard. The double standard, which is still very common among whites, allowed premarital and extramarital sexual expression for men and denied it to women. But some women had to serve as sexual objects for the liberated white male, and black women were forced to take this role.†

* Random House, Canada, 1972.
† Staples, Robert. "Mystique of Black Sexuality," *The Black Family*. Belmont, CA: Wadsworth Publishing Co., 1971, pg. 119.

How then can we discuss *In Defense of Ourselves* with a particular approach that is distinctly the black perspective for women. It presents a challenge to merge cultural differences with the needs and similarity for defense of all women in relation to forcible rape.

If one views race in a modern, current perspective, black women come in all ages, physical statures and conditions, economic circumstances and educational backgrounds. Because of the variety of individual circumstances, acculturation and personal preparation, one would assume a vast degree of difference in the individual black woman's ability to communicate and to defend herself with a potential rapist and to succeed. The one strong bond with these women is their black cultural and racial heritage and its effect on their identity development. This is uniquely theirs and is a positive bond that binds them together from generation to generation in a continuing line of expectation of strength while adapting to an "outside" alien and oppressive society.

The subject of rape is especially potent in the light of American history and current role expectations and status given to black women. It immediately stirs up incredible feelings of distaste, anger and defensiveness. Sex is presently seen in this culture as a pleasurable experience with a partner of choice, not with someone who is totally immersed in his own unhealthy needs.

The feelings of anger, aggression or defensiveness do not necessarily mean that the black woman is automatically prepared to defend herself. Most black women, however, have a psychological aversion and healthy paranoia toward *anyone* who may tamper with her survival. From early childhood, most black women find themselves in conventional non-permissive families. They are especially conditioned to be wary of white males in general social encounters and are taught by parents and by experience to expect a possible negative encounter. In addition, in many instances the black woman, as a more equal participant than her white counterpart in the economic struggles in the extended family, is *taught* to be more independent in her dealings with *all* males. She is, in fact, conditioned to be a strong contributor, a supporter, a source of strength and affection in a flexible family unit and often becomes the glue that binds the family unit together.

If we view rape with the above perception of the role of a black woman, we might come to some conclusions. In connection with rape prevention, the black woman, as seen from the majority "political" or "societal" perspective, would appear to be conditioned to be the "victim." If we view the strong potential and training within the family unit in the Black Experience, or the "personal" view and regard the black woman as strong, independent and wary, we would consider her as a good candidate for survival or coping positively with a rape situation. As the author stated, "How good you feel about yourself will directly dictate how you will defend yourself." Black women have an opportunity to defend themselves as well as shrewd assessment abilities to discern a different and dangerous adversary.

In addition to the basic positive and independent characteristics of the black woman, it is imperative that assertive techniques as outlined in the book—such as body language, eye contact, tone of voice and language use—be reassessed to conform with the personality characteristics of the black woman according to class, education, etc. It is imperative that an *assertive* message rather than a negative-aggressive message be given to the potential rapist. If the black woman uses the strengths that are a part of her conditioning process, including the ability to be an assured "lady," then this book can be of invaluable assistance in providing protection. Role playing and practicing of self-defense approaches is essential so that automatic reactions may be *expected* from the black woman toward a potential rapist.

In a historical and a current sense, it must be remembered that few people other than family have been interested in the welfare of the black woman. Her working conditions, protection in traveling, location of living quarters and economic situation often place her in a vulnerable position. She cannot count on anyone to be responsible *for* her. She must rely on her own abilities to be responsible for her own fate and her ability to adequately defend herself.

Her vulnerability can be countered with her shrewd abilities to survive against difficult odds. *In Defense of Ourselves* helps to provide this empowerment in an organized, positive way, taking into account the special characteristics and strengths of the black woman. The book provides her with a meaningful tool to cope with one of the most negative and distasteful social situations in today's society.

Asian Women

by Elaine Kanzaki Wong

Elaine Kanzaki Wong is a Sansei (third-generation Japanese-American) married to a first-generation Chinese-American and the mother of two children. She is a member of the Asian/Pacific Women's Caucus and the Pierce County Women's Coalition.

Some background is needed to state that when I talk about Asian/Pacific people today residing in the United States, I am talking about multiple ethnic groups. As late as the 1950s, three ethnic groups dominated what was then considered "Oriental Minorities." These were peoples whose native land was China, Japan or the Philippines. But since the early fifties, Asian people can very well be immigrants from the three countries mentioned above, as well as Korea, Vietnam, Cambodia, Laos, Thailand, Guam, Samoa, Fiji and others.

Although I have had contact with foreign-born Asian and Pacific Island women, I have not worked extensively with them. Therefore, the following general views, although they *may* apply across the board to all Asian/Pacific women, are not intended as such, but instead are my personal views presented by me.

It would be foolhardy for anyone to try to speak on behalf of all these diverse countries and cultures, but as an Asian-American woman, I do find that there are consistent stereotypes which are perpetuated about all of us, lumping us under one banner.

In considering media stereotypes, one of the first things that comes to mind is the concept of "exotic." Adult Asian/Pacific women are usually portrayed as strikingly beautiful, mysterious, intriguing and sexy, which is often coupled with the notion that she is also readily available. The movies made just after World War II are horrendous examples of Asian women in occupied Japan. So eager to become Americanized, they awkwardly dance to boogie-woogie beats while spouting such stock phrases as "Hey, G.I., wanta have a good time?" (in broken English, of course).

Even movies made much later, such as *South Pacific* and *Teahouse of the August Moon*, showed Asian/Pacific women as give-away gifts. France Nuyen portrays an innocent, charming young woman who is openly offered as a gift to a foot soldier (Pfc.) by her guardian, Bloody Mary. In *Teahouse*, the character of Lotus Blossom is expected to serve, dress and wait on the lieutenant to whom she is presented as a gift. Many double entendres are used in explanation of the supposedly awkward situation the lieutenant finds himself in—because she is also expected to sleep with him.

What does this have to do with rape? The notion that Asian women are eager to bed down with American G.I.s for love, money, status or, in the case of Susie in *The World of Susie Wong*, to support an aging parent and a sick child, can lead the audience to only one conclusion. For whatever the reason, whatever the plot, there's always room for the dedicated rapist in Asian countries.

The fact that so many movies show Asian women and white American G.I.s in either potential rape scenes or out-and-out solicitation for sex is indicative of the relationship the United States and its representative (the G.I.) has had with Asian countries since 1940, i.e., the vanquisher versus the vanquished.

Powerful American men, who are the decision makers in the military and in government, like their counterparts in Asian countries, are seldom shown. The war is played out between the white foot soldier (or war correspondent in the case of William Holden in *Love Is a Many Splendored Thing*), and the Asian woman in Hong Kong, Okinawa or *somewhere* in the South Pacific.

These movies are about Asian women in their own home countries. What happens when Hollywood attempts to portray Asian-American women living in San Francisco's Chinatown? We are portrayed in cutesy, toe-tapping numbers like *Flower Drum Song*. Here we find three different views of Asian women. First, the older Chinese mother who is "put-down" by her jive-speaking teen-age children as old-fashioned and uncool. Secondly, there is the chosen bride who comes from the "old country" to marry the eldest son, and she too is a loser and an anachronism. Only the third characterization, played by Nancy Kwan, emerges as a winner. She is the swinging, hip cutie, who works in a night club as a stripper. The message again is all too obvious . . . bad, sexy, loose Asian woman gets her man, the hero!

When we talk of violence and its overall effect on our individual sensitivities, as well as the adverse effect it has on our youth, we must not forget what took place over every network TV station night after night, month after month, during the late sixties and early seventies.

Each night our local TV news station would bring vivid atrocities in living color, right into our homes, in their coverage of the Vietnam war. Over and over, we would witness bombing and strafing of Vietnamese villages and women and children running for their lives, in some instances covered with flaming napalm. So frequently were we accosted by these spectacles that even the most sensitive viewer could find herself occasionally lapsing into a state where viewing live on-the-spot coverage could be confused momentarily with fiction. If this be the case, what of the rapist(s) viewing these same violent shows?

Although NBC and CBS didn't cover raping and pillaging of these villages (TV news is, after all, rated G), it takes little imagination to know that much of this took place. We have all seen the movie where raping and pillaging are glorified and excused. A film whose rationale seems to be something like, "Well, these soldier boys are horny and those blankety-blanks are the enemy and get what they deserve." These films show troops of victorious soldiers taking over a village after a hard-won battle, where, incidentally, at least two of the well-known actors have been wounded or killed, thereby gaining the audience's sympathy, no matter what follows. They proceed to rough up some of the villagers, and end up grabbing the nearest female. Then we have a typical Hollywood fade-out as she is struggling in vain. Furthermore, we are always shown these Asian women, children and old men left alone in the village "deserted" by their men. The implication is clear . . . these cowardly Asian men have left their women and children helpless victims to be "taken" by the first comers. Has anyone wondered how long these people have been widowed and orphaned because their men might have been killed months ago?

Advertising media uses the Asian woman as sex objects to sell perfumes (Jade East, Hai Karate, etc.), clothing (kimonos, sarongs, cheong-sans), and trips to the Orient (Northwest Airlines, Pan Am and travel brochures showing half-clad, flower-bedecked Pacific Island women). But the most insidious usage of Asian women is in weekly TV shows such as *Hawaii Five-O*. Here we are shown as vacuous, empty-headed, doll-like creatures, fawning over Jack Lord, who plays a character that is the typical, hard-nosed, gun-slinging, violent detective.

Suffice it to say that the Asian woman in media, be it movies, TV, advertising or music (remember Poor Butterfly, 'neath the blossoms waiting), is grossly one-dimensional. There seems to be no attempt to present the Asian woman in any other light. Why? Is it for male ego gratification? Is it lack of exposure to true understanding of the strength and abilities of Asian women? Is it because this image pays off at the box office? Your guess is as good as mine—because few of us truly fit the stereotype presented, and none of us fit it entirely!

The chapter on "American Etiquette" has application, I believe, for *any* female growing up in America, regardless of her ethnicity. There are additions of a few specifics that may apply to Asian women.

It is my feeling that many foreign-born women might react to a male "come-on" or indirect solicitation with confusion due to lack of facility with the English language, especially slang terminology. The manifestation of her own bewilderment at not knowing what is being said to her might be the embarrassed giggle or a shy smile. This reaction plays directly into the expectations of the male, be he a potential rapist or not. It reinforces all of his stereotypic views. Even the automatic response of covering one's mouth with one's hand hearkens up World War II films of embarrassed geishas upon seeing their first hairy-chested Caucasian, as in the movie *My Geisha*.

Asian women born and raised in this country understand at an early age that male children are somehow valued more than female children. We are conditioned to respect males and not be assertive toward them. We are taught the notion that *they* know what is right for *us*. Beyond the usual conditioning, Asian-Americans are expected, as racial minority people, to act nice to all those people who are seemingly nice to them. Some of us have been told, for example, that "some white people will judge *all* Asian-Americans by *your* behavior, so be on your best behavior at all times."

Occasionally, Asian women meet men who are what I dub "Oriental-philes." These men claim to be enamored of everything oriental, i.e., the artwork, classic paintings, pottery, enamelware, clothing and various ancient artifacts. In short, they admire everything about the culture and, of course, that includes Oriental women. Because so much is presented as negative in the stereotypes about

Asians, the Asian woman finds herself distinctly vulnerable in this positive stereotype situation and may respond positively when she might be better off to respond negatively. Is she not, after all, being regarded as another oriental *objet d'art*? Each one of us must decide for herself when confronted by this special situation.

As I look at the chapter, "Self-concept," I realize again that what is being said here applies to all women. I would add the dimension of physical self-concept as it uniquely applies to non-white women.

I am reminded of the fact that as an Asian woman growing up in a Caucasion host culture, most standards of beauty don't apply to me. I cannot look like Farrah Fawcett-Majors, for example, even if I buy a blond wig and some false teeth. Or for that matter how does the average adolescent Asian girl relate to the breast-centered *Playboy* image?

I'm implying that if one's physical self-image is not positive (especially in a society where how you look and smell is more important than how much you know), then intrinsic feelings of self-worth will also not be positive. Just as feminists have demanded that women be viewed as occupying many and varied positions in our society rather than only in the kitchen cooking, cleaning and scrubbing, Asian women too must be seen in multi-dimensional roles. Maybe media will one day become so sophisticated that even an Asian can be the one on a commercial who has bad breath!

In reading through "Seven Exercises," I find that it does have application for me as an Asian-American woman who was reared in a large Midwestern city and who had to become acquainted very early in life with the idea of taking care of myself.

There are some Asian/Pacific women who might find the "I" concept more difficult to relate to because they see themselves as very much a part of a societal "we"; but then, perhaps a book such as this one, translated in many Asian languages, would be just the right learning tool to begin to change the "we" to "I." Use of the "First Thoughts" exercises, with special attention paid to the "*I* want to be around tomorrow because . . ." statement may be especially useful.

I have one parting piece of information to share concerning the chapter on physical self-defense. In the early seventies, a relatively unknown actor by the name of Bruce Lee emerged on the popular film scene in Chinese martial-art films. And for the first time the general American audience got a glimpse of the type of films Chinese residing in populous Chinatowns throughout the nation were enjoying on a weekly basis.

Bruce Lee was a second-generation Chinese-American, bilingual and able to bridge two cultures. He popularized the Kung Fu martial-arts style. Although Bruce Lee represented, for many of us, a long-awaited image of positive, strong Asian male, the women in his films (which focused on *him* as a superstar), played minor and supportive roles, often damsels in distress. This is in *sharp* contrast to films produced in Hong Kong and Taiwan for Chinese-speaking audiences only, in which women and men are portrayed as equally strong in the martial arts. Furthermore, women are often shown as leaders and the unsung heroines of traditional Chinese folklore.

In summary, I believe that rape prevention is a reality for all Asian/Pacific women. It is a necessary survival tool for us. Keeping in mind some of the specific conditioning we have been exposed to, we can apply this workbook to our own lives and, along with our many other Asian/Pacific women, learn and grow to be free from the fear of rape.

Chicana Women

by Patricia Benavídez

Patricia Benavídez is a former elementary school physical education specialist. Presently she is involved working full time on women's issues in the political, educational and organizational arenas.

The Chicana, like her sisters of all racial, ethnic and cultural groups, has not escaped the blatant physical and sexual abuse perpetrated against all women.

The Chicana, whether she lives in the urban or rural area, has been subject to rape. Like her sisters of other cultures, Chicanas have lived in fear of the repercussions of what happens to them if they report the fact that they have been sexually and physically abused. Chicanas face the turmoil of being castigated by their families as unworthy and promiscuous and not living up to the "cult of virginity." The implied message is that the woman is at fault, that she asked for it and that she should have known better than to be out by herself.

The police are generally never utilized because the Chicana often views the harassment of the police as worse violence than the actual rape itself. It's like piling violence on violence. Often because of language differences the Chicana is unable to participate fully in her own behalf because she does not understand or is not given assistance in the process of securing justice for herself.

The emotional experience of being subjected to what may perhaps be her first pelvic exam as a result of having reported the rape brings great psychological trauma to the Chicana. Counseling centers where the Chicana may be able to receive sensitive assistance and emotional support are almost non-existent. A Chicana staff is generally absent at the many centers that do exist.

Consequently, the incidence of rape among Chicanas is largely unknown. We do know, however, that the incidence of rape in the Chicana community is much higher than any statistics may reveal. It was not until the now-famous Inez Garcia case that Chicanas and other Spanish-speaking women began to assert themselves in defense against the violence thrust upon them, and the issue of rape and rape prevention has focused attention as an issue facing Chicanas. The silence has been broken.

Because Chicanas work in concentrated areas where security is minimal—and often live in neighborhoods labeled unsafe—it behooves us, along with other women, to learn about how we can take control of our lives and be able to defend ourselves against physical and sexual abuse.

It is appropriate, then, that any book dealing with the issue of rape prevention consider the sociological and psychological foundations that have facilitated the vulnerability of Chicanas to sexual and physical violence.

The machismo syndrome needs to be addressed in terms of the reality of how Chicanas have been victimized by the very protection that machismo supposedly provides her. The Chicano male is reared from early childhood to accept the dominant role in his relationship to women. His virility is viewed and reinforced by the culture to serve as the protector, provider and defender of the Chicana.

The young Chicana learns never to question her father, uncles or brothers, even if the brother happens to be younger than she. She is expected to not look at males directly in the eye. Chicanas are constantly reminded that they must always be in the company of a man. Even in adulthood, many Chicanas are not allowed by their husbands to go anywhere by themselves. Consequently, Chicanas frequently do not have the opportunity to develop skills that would help them to cope with attacks when they are alone. The woman living under this pattern never develops her own selfhood. When the myth that she will always be protected crumbles, the Chicana finds that she has not taken the steps to develop the skills to help her fend for herself and take charge of her own life.

The self-concept of the Chicana has been demeaned not only within the context of her own ethnic culture, but from the insensitivity of institutionalized racism in this society. A Chicana's self-concept is the victim of the "double whammy."

The insensitivity of the racist society is manifested and perpetuated in the educational system in various ways.

Language: Her linguistic difference is rarely acknowledged as an asset or a skill to value and retain. More often than not this difference is viewed as a handicap, and the message perceived by the non-English speaker is that "something must be wrong with you" because you do not speak the "right" language. This negation of one's primary language is perpetuated through comments such as, "I learned to speak English, why can't you?" On the other hand, the assumption is often made that Spanish speakers do not develop a command of English. An example of this is illustrated by a comment made to a Chicana colleague after a presentation she had made at a national conference. An Anglo male approached her and said, "You speak very good English for a Mexican."

Textbooks and curriculum materials: Chicanas rarely see themselves portrayed other than in stereotypical roles. Their cultural heritage and contributions are rarely included as part of their curriculum. Similarly, Chicanas are grossly underrepresented in educational positions in comparison to their numbers in the population. Chicanas have not had the opportunity of experiencing positive-role models in education, either through their teachers or administrators. It is not uncommon for a young Chicana to proceed through her whole education without having the benefit of being taught by a single Chicana.

Physical activity: The area of developing a positive attitude toward one's body and physical strength has been largely ignored in terms of the Chicana. Opportunity for participating in sports and other physical activity has not been provided for the young Chicana. Chicanas are generally not exposed to physical education programs until junior high.

The assertiveness training concepts and exercises detailed by this book are applicable to the Chicana, just as they are to all women. However, it is crucial to remember that as the Chicana asserts her demands for her equity as a woman, the change that is involved must be from within her own cultural frame of reference, which stands within the context of a racist society. While the Chicana shares in the victimization of all women, her own unique needs, interests and values are not necessarily those of the majority culture.

Chicanas can also profit from the self-defense exercises suggested. Consideration must be given to assisting the Chicana in developing skills not only to protect herself from attack, but to initially develop a sense of pride in having control of her own physical strength and power as it relates to all areas of her life. Self-defense begins in the mind. Thus, if the Chicana has been provided support from her cultural frame of reference, she will have an effective rationale that learning self-defense is not making her a "man hater," but is teaching her to protect herself.

Native American Women

by Carol DuShane

Carol DuShane is the counselor at an all-Indian high school in Seattle, and herself a Crow Indian. She works with urban Indian teen-agers and their families. She makes no attempt to speak for Native American women in general, but has strong feelings on the subject of rape, particularly regarding its relationship to the subject of self-determination.

One thing women—and we are the majority—and ethnic minorities have in common is our second-class-citizen status: our relative lack of power compared to white men to affect our environments and to control our lives.

For Indians such a state of affairs is a direct result of the coming of the white man. When certain power-hungry whites began pushing the Indian west in the name of Manifest Destiny, it was much more than land that was being taken away. In the ensuing power struggle the Indian came out the loser. What the reservation system and the Bureau of Indian Affairs attempted to create was a system where the Native American was isolated and totally dependent on the "great white father" for everything—food, shelter, medical care. In other words, a system in which the Native American was totally powerless—and then expected to be grateful.

From this position of no responsibility/no control, much like the position of childhood, it is a short step to the position of victim. The "benevolent" white guardian quickly and easily becomes the persecutor, in the form of the B.I.A. boarding school, the white cop, the F.B.I., the welfare department, the court system, the white school system, even the social worker and the missionary. Victimization becomes the expected and ordinary state of affairs.

Contrary to the messages of her traditional upbringing to be proud and strong, it isn't surprising that a Native American woman may feel herself in the position of victim and powerless to do anything to change that. Perhaps even more than her white sister, her experience is almost entirely with an external control system: parents, schools, B.I.A., the welfare system, etc. It seems that somebody outside is always in charge of what happens to her.

Like other women, the Indian woman hears the messages of the media and the prevailing culture, and compounded with her own cultural conflicts this may intensify her feelings that she is helpless and dependent. Given the circumstance of a power play with a man—be he husband or rapist—it is easy to feel that this is one more instance in a life that "happens to me and over which I have little control; the world is a scary place and I need someone to take care of me, because I can't take care of myself." The "Self-concept" chapter is particularly useful in learning some of the ways we tell ourselves that we're victims and powerless, and ways to get over feeling like that.

We are not weak and defenseless women. Native Americans are strong people —we would not have survived at all were that not the case. Indian women are particularly strong—physically and emotionally. Many live to be wise, truly inspirational old women. Traditional Indians were and are the center and strength of the family, which often means supporting and literally holding things together.

We are strong women, and we need not give away our power to anyone. It is only when we buy the myths that we are weak and the world is a scary place and the only refuge is a man to take care of us, that we become the world's victims.

Women do need men; and men, women. People need one another, and that in itself does not spell weakness. But before we can freely relate to any other person, we must have a sense of our own strength and worth. We must be able to depend on ourselves—to defend ourselves if need be—because we see ourselves as worthwhile persons deserving not just to live but to live well.

In order to make that happen for ourselves, we must start with our own bodies. We must get in touch with our own power and pride, and learn to stop giving that away.

This book begins with describing the influences that lead women to become "sweet young things"—fragile flowers, so to speak—which is another way of saying "potential rape victims." It goes on to do much more than give tips on how to "be careful." It suggests ways to change the very attitude that lead us to see ourselves as helpless victims. Again, the "Self-concept" chapter and the exercises described there, and the assertiveness training exercises can be very helpful in teaching us to overcome our notion of ourselves as victims.

For me, this is the crucial thing. When I believe that I have options other than lamenting the dangers I face as a woman—when I see that I have other options besides just "running scared"—when I believe in myself and in my strength and abilities, then I am an equal of all men, and *anyone* will have trouble making me a victim. I think this book shows some specific ways for me and all women to learn how to make those options real in our lives.

Battered Women

by Katrin E. Frank

Katrin E. Frank is the co-ordinator of the Evergreen Legal Services' Abused Women Project, which has existed in Seattle since May 1976. The project considers a woman abused if she has been the object of threats, violence or crimes against her property.

There are many similarities between the victims of rape and the victims of other forms of abuse. The first half of this book describes how women become vulnerable; how we are set up to become victims. The things that make women vulnerable to rape also make them vulnerable to abuse.

However, there are some significant differences in society's view of rapists and rape victims, and current attitudes toward abusers and abused women. The authors of this book say that society does not approve of rape. While the way rape is presented in movies and the media leaves a lot to be desired, at least rape is given a negative value. There is at least some minimal interest in bringing the rapist to justice.

This is not so in the case of abuse. How many times have we seen a man hit, choke, or slap a woman on television or in the movies? How often have we seen a man condemned or punished for such an act? There do not appear to be any consequences for such acts.

In real life, the situation is as portrayed in the media. When someone sees a man beating a woman, he or she usually looks away. When the police respond to calls from victims, they try to defuse the situation. They frequently say there is nothing further they can do, and they rarely make an arrest. The woman is left with the feeling that there is no help for her, and that others do not view the abuse as serious or harmful to her. And the abusive man sees no negative consequences to his act. No one tells the woman that she doesn't have to put up with it. There seems to be no sympathy for her and no way out.

Where there are special projects, abused women are learning they have rights, and the police are becoming more responsive to the victims.

Many people have been unsympathetic to battered women for several reasons. If a woman remains in an abusive relationship, it is viewed as her problem: "She must really like it or she'd leave; she must provoke it; she probably deserves it; it turns her on." Not only the public, but also the abusers and victims need to be made aware that abuse is a problem and abusive conduct is criminal.

Why do women stay in abusive relationships? Why do they put up with black eyes, concussions, miscarriages and broken bones? The chapters "American Etiquette" and "Self-concept" give a partial answer. We reach adulthood with low self-esteem. We are encouraged to be passive, financially dependent. We are taught that we should not win encounters with men. We think time spent with us is a favor. We learn to be defined by our relationships with men. We lose confidence in our physical abilities. We feel a lack of control over our destiny. Lack of self-sufficiency and feelings of inadequacy make it difficult for a woman to leave an abusive relationship. Without a clear sense that she is being mistreated, a woman is even less likely to leave.

In some cases of abuse the victim and assailant are married or live together. Often the victim cares for her assailant. In many cases, after an assault has taken place, the man apologizes and promises it will never happen again. This tends to encourage a woman to stick it out. She may not report abuse because she feels that she would be betraying her husband. The security of the known, painful as it is, is less terrifying than the unknown.

We are all vulnerable to abuse and can benefit from the assertiveness training techniques described in this book. Women who are in an abuse situation need the exercises that will develop self-confidence. They need to learn that they do not have to be victims. Men who hit women choose their victims just as rapists do. If a woman likes herself and is self-confident, she is less likely to become a victim of abuse. And if she is a victim, she can change her situation. It is not an easy task, and a woman is not stupid or lazy or hopeless if she is unable to stop being abused. There are many variables, and no one should set herself or himself up to judge what a woman should do in such a situation.

There are also severely disturbed men who will batter no matter what. Men convicted of assault don't necessarily discontinue assaultive behavior. However, these men are not in the majority, and as with rapists, the behavior of the victim can have an effect on the situation.

The early sections of this book are an excellent discussion of how we become vulnerable. The exercises that deal with body language, eye contact, tone of voice, assertive sentence structure and the chart of timid, hostile and assertive responses are all useful to abused and potentially abused women. The exercises that suggest reasons we should care about ourselves and keep ourselves in good health are particularly relevant to abused women. I would also suggest that women who have children try another exercise. Remind yourself that children often grow up to repeat the actions and behavior of their parents. List the reactions your children observe in a battering situation. Look at the list. Are there things you hope your children won't do or say? Try to change those things in your own reactions. You *can* change your responses. Your children will definitely benefit in the long run if you feel better about your actions in such a situation.

Abused women are especially responsive to the support of other women. Rap groups for abused women are a recent development. Both the women in the groups and the leaders have stated emphatically how supportive and helpful these groups are and how dramatic the changes are that take place in a relatively short period of time. Obviously, changes do not take place overnight, but support from other women in a difficult and frightening period has given many women the strength to make changes they were unable to make on their own.

There is a real question whether abused women should use the self-defense techniques of the book, especially when they intend to continue the relationship. I would be extremely unlikely to gouge my husband's eyes or hit him in the nose. If I do these things to him and we stay together, he undoubtedly will beat me more severely the next time.

I do not mean to say that women shouldn't defend themselves when attacked. But I do think there are different considerations if you are assaulted by someone you care for or will have to continue living with.

This book is an excellent tool for women who are working with abused women. It gives a clear picture of how women can become victims and why they might stay in an abusive relationship. The exercises to develop self-confidence and assertiveness are good. We are not stupid if we become victims; we are not hopeless if we cannot stop being victimized. The techniques in this book if used with young women can help prevent them from becoming victims of abuse. For women who are abused, I would emphasize the necessity of the support of other women. I would also emphasize Exercise I—to encourage feelings of self-value and safety—and Exercises II through V. Abused women can make up their own "What-if Games." They can set up situations that they know usually lead to a fight. All these exercises can work well in groups. But if a group is not available, a woman can work on them by herself.

Many women wish to maintain the relationship they are in but wish to stop the abuse. This may be difficult to accomplish alone. If the man also wishes to stop the abuse, the couple can work at it together and seek outside help. There is a good likelihood that abuse can stop. If a woman wishes to stop the abusive behavior herself and the man does not admit it is a problem, it is more difficult to stop. I recommend that the woman seek out other women to work with. Once an abused woman learns she has options, she can choose to exercise them or not. But she will have a tool to work with by using this book.

Abuse prevention is a large topic. There is the prevention before it happens, which can be dealt with the same way as rape prevention. But there is also abuse prevention when a woman is in an on-going relationship. The end results may be different. This book is a useful guide for prevention of abuse in both cases.

We need to know how easily we can become victims. And we need to learn that we can control ourselves and our destinies.

Past Victims of Sexual Abuse

by Connie Murphy

Connie Murphy is the Advocate Director of the Pierce County Rape Relief. She has volunteered in the treatment program of Western State Hospital's Sexual Offenders program. She is currently co-facilitating a teen-age incest-victims group.

There are two forms of sexual abuse that I will discuss. The first is rape; the second is child sexual abuse—incest and child molestation. My interest and involvement with incest victims came about as a result of my work with the rape-crisis line. As a rape-crisis counselor, I met with incest victims. One example was the adult woman, a recent rape victim, who was catapulted into her incestuous past by the rape. To this woman, the similarities between the rape and the incest were all too obvious.

I've counseled several women in the past year whose rapes were considered "questionable" and were often labeled "promiscuous" by the authorities. At first, it stunned me to discover the number of these women who were incest victims and who inevitably turned their conversation away from the rape and to the incest. I found many of these so-called "promiscuous" women confused over the definition and dynamics of rape, confused over their ability or option to say "no." The word "no" had not been an option in their incestuous pasts. The major male authority figure in their lives (either father or stepfather) had taken this option as his right.

Another example is the incest victim who calls the rape-crisis center in her first attempts to move out of the incestuous situation. Her desires to be free of the incest are complicated by her fears and her need to protect her family. She is in the process of taking control of her life and demanding that her needs be recognized. This will not come easily to the young incest victim. Her feelings about herself and her worth are negligible at this time.

The victim of incest, like the rape victim, feels somehow responsible for the incest. Despite the cultural and social victimization of women, we are led to believe that some protection is offered by the family. We learn very early that the offender is someone outside the family, perhaps a stranger offering candy, but never our own brothers or fathers. When the victims of incest learn from their peers that other families differ from their own, they assume a great deal of guilt and anger. But these feelings are generally subdued.

As the incest victim learns self-assertion, she hopefully learns that she is not responsible for the feelings and actions of others. I see the victims of incest struggling continually with their need to feel responsible for others. *In Defense of Ourselves* discusses the learning that goes on in our society which centers a woman's attentions on the needs and concerns of others. This learning pattern is doubly reinforced for a woman in the incestuous family. The incestuous father or stepfather has often kept his daughter docile with the belief that by giving in to his demands, she is keeping the family together and protecting him and the family. The role of family caretaker is further extended in the confusion of roles between the mother and the incest victim. The victim replaces her mother not only in her father's bed, but in the homemaking and care of siblings. For most women, childhood is a period of their lives in which they need not yet concern themselves with the importance of others. This period is rather significantly shortened for the victim of incest.

The role of family caretaker can often lead to life-styles that continue the pattern of victimization and exploitation. Studies done in prisons show correlations between chronic runaways, prostitution, drug abuse and incidences of child sexual abuse.

It is important to identify the types of intervention that will most benefit the individual. The intervention should not only be supportive, but alternatives should be relayed that will increase the victim's scope of choices and provide tools that will enable her to follow through on those choices.

Two of the primary objectives of the incest-victim rap groups that I presently work with are building of self-esteem and developing assertiveness skills. These two components are important to the victim's safety if she returns to the home. We teach these components through discussion, role-plays, assertiveness exercises and by creating an atmosphere where it is safe to try on several alternatives.

The main thrust of *In Defense of Ourselves* is very much in harmony with the objectives of the teen-age incest-victim rap group and could easily be incorporated into the work already done with the group. Chapters I and II might be broken down for discussion over a period of weeks and integrated with the exercises from Chapter IV.

The first chapter of the book deals with movies and the media, which continue to represent women in roles that maintain the myth of woman as victim. I believe that much of this chapter is beyond the sophistication of the teen-age victims I work with. These teen-agers, as most teen-agers, are chronic consumers of this media and simply do not care how women are represented.

This chapter on media would work well with a group of adult rape victims who are "forced" to an awareness of the second-class status of women throughout our culture. Exploration of the media, as in Chapter I, would aid these women in understanding the "whys" of rape (a question that is difficult to resolve for the rape victim). It is important to recognize that deviant sexual behavior is learned behavior, and as Sanford and Fetter mention very early in their book, much of our learning is done through the visual media. The sexual offender believes adamantly in the sex role stereotyping and myths that are prevalent throughout our media.

The exercises that are discussed in Chapter IV would work easily with the objectives of the incest-victim rap groups, because they deal with self-concept and provide new ways to respond to situations. "First Thoughts" is an excellent warm-up for a group such as this and sets the tone for the positive self-assertions that should come out of the group experience. The following four chapters might be used as tools in reviewing what constitutes the assertive stance: body posture, eye contact and voice level. The exercises themselves are not sufficient to generate assertiveness, but can be reinforced with role-plays of situations from the victim's life.

As the victims' awareness of their own worth grows, their anger will certainly rise. It should be recognized and supported, but alternative ways of relating to people must be defined and modeled. The incest victim has grown up in a family where the only alternatives in relationships have been either a passive or aggressive response. There is a third alternative, assertiveness, and the book explores the differences between these three responses. What is most important is that the reader can view the consequences of each response and identify the advantages of the assertive response.

The chapter on etiquette and courtesy is a relevant area to explore with the incest and rape victims. The women often come from homes that are restrictive, with the rules of courtesy helping to maintain the clearly defined male and female roles, (the female role being most specifically one of victim). Before the incest becomes known to the community, the incest victim is often seen as a "well-behaved" child. This could be a synonym for "passive." The rules listed in "American Etiquette" would be points for discussion especially when contrasted with the rights that the victims learn to define as their own. If the discussion of the rules was to progress, I feel that role-plays could be integrated into the discussion. For example, if the group is discussing Rule Two ("We Must Always Answer a Question that Is Asked of Us"), then several situations might be presented to the group for response. The victims then could practice alternative ways of responding and discover which response is best for them.

The physical exercises can also play an important role for young women who have learned that physical contact can lead easily to sex. The ability to defend themselves physically has never seemed to be a realistic alternative when responding to their fathers. The story is told of the young incest victim who explained that she indeed had defended herself against her father. On further inquiry, it was learned that the victim's concept of defending herself had been to hold on tightly to the bedpost as her father approached her.

The incest-victim rap groups have T-shirts upon which is printed, "My body belongs to me." Despite the slogan, I think practicing self-defense and exploring their body strengths would be entirely new to them. I appreciate the fact that *In Defense of Ourselves* discusses self-defense techniques in a realistic fashion, identifying the limits and advantages of the various schools. When self-defense has been discussed in the group in the past, it has been in unrealistic, movie-world terms, not as a reality for the group. After reading *In Defense of Ourselves*, I have considered offering a self-defense class specifically for the victim rap groups.

Other books in the past have offered a look at the patterns of victimization in our culture but have not concerned themselves with what women might do to break these patterns. I believe that all women, whether they have been physically assaulted or not, could benefit from reading this book. I hope that as more schools offer self-defense classes in their curriculums for women, they will take a look at a more conclusive way of teaching these classes. This book would be an excellent tool in a curriculum. Also, I think that the victim rap groups (whether rape or incest) could easily make use of the book. As we identify areas of victimization and exploitation and teach women that they need not accept this for their lives, then perhaps more incest and rape victims will come forward to demand the help they need.

Developmentally Disabled Women

by *Laurie Gates, M.S.W.*

Laurie Gates is an experienced therapist presently working with developmentally disabled clients at the Tacoma Goodwill Industries Rehabilitation Center.

I have been asked to write a critique on how *In Defense of Ourselves* applies to a specific population group: developmentally disabled women. In the forthcoming pages, my use of the term "developmentally disabled" will be restricted to those individuals with limited intellectual potential, or mental retardation of a mild to moderate level.* My profession is social work, and at the time of this writing I am employed by Tacoma Goodwill Industries Rehabilitation Center. This agency is dedicated to providing training and rehabilitation services, including vocational, personal and social adjustment, to individuals with developmental, psychological and physical disabilities. Among the social and personal adjustment services offered are groups dealing with areas such as sexuality, self-awareness and assertiveness. Based on assessment of client need, training in these areas appears to be very necessary, and the information presented in *In Defense of Ourselves* may be very useful in planning and implementing means for meeting these needs. Rape has been a problem for some developmentally disabled women, and rape prevention is one goal of our awareness training.

This book applies to developmentally disabled women just as it applies to all other women. A continuum of personalities, problem-solving skills and emotional sensitivity is seen in developmentally disabled women as in all other women. However, there are some general characteristics and specific needs particularly evident in developmentally disabled women that are addressed by this book but would require some modification for application.

Through reading the book, several trends emerge that seem to have implications for developmentally disabled women. First of all, assertiveness and self-

* Mental retardation is generally categorized into the following functional levels based on I.Q. scores:

I.Q. 55–69 Mild Retardation
    40–54 Moderate Retardation
    25–39 Severe Retardation
     0–24 Profound Retardation

My comments will reflect my experience with individuals at the mild and moderate levels only.

image directly affect the way a woman will respond in an assault or potential assault situation. Also, the media, along with etiquette "shoulds" (in Chapter II), go a long way toward influencing our assertive skills and self-image by modeling passive/submissive sex-role stereotypes in relationships and assault situations. Additionally, stereotypes of classic rape situations do not reflect average real-life rape situations, making it more difficult for any woman to define a dating situation, for example, as having potential for assault. It is that much more difficult for a developmentally disabled woman to make this differentiation, due to several sociological and developmental factors.

In the above areas, the developmentally disabled woman is strongly impacted because of many factors. First of all, in addition to being trained in the traditional female role, developmentally disabled women have also often been treated as children all their lives, leading to even *greater* development of a passive/submissive role. Many parents of developmentally disabled children, especially female, seem to overprotect their daughters and expect less from them than they are truly capable of producing. For example, some parents assume that their mildly affected daughter will never live independently, marry, or work in a competitive job. These beliefs have been proven invalid time and time again, and the protective attitude usually tends to result in a self-fulfilling prophecy if the daughter is not allowed to work toward achieving her full potential. This overprotectiveness also contributes to the development of low self-esteem and submissive behavior, as well as frequently limiting knowledge of basic sexual facts and personal sexual awareness. All of this affects the way a developmentally disabled woman will perceive and respond to a sexual-assault situation.

Additionally, the impact of television is especially strong, since developmentally disabled persons seem to watch much TV, especially those living in institutional or semi-institutional settings. Also, ability to use abstract reasoning and judgment regarding the validity of implied TV-role messages is limited, increasing the chances of the passive/submissive female-role model being taken on without questioning.

Let's look at a hypothetical case of a developmentally disabled woman in a potential assault situation. Kim, a twenty-one-year-old, mildly retarded woman, has just moved from her parents' home to her own apartment. She has had no sexual experience and has been told the "facts of life." But she has not been told how sex fits into a relationship. She meets a neighbor, Bill, who lives alone upstairs and is about twenty-six. He begins to visit her often with the excuse of borrowing kitchen items. He says flattering words to her and gives her attention she has not had from a man before. He begins to make sexual advances and eventually requests that she have intercourse with him. Kim has begun to like Bill very much and wants to do anything to please him. She does not clearly understand what he wants to do with her, but senses it is something she should not do. However, she does not want to anger Bill, and he is very insistent. She becomes very confused, and then frightened when he begins removing her clothes, but she submits to the situation. Afterward, Bill is nice to her, but leaves quickly. Kim is left alone feeling scared and hurt and not understanding what just happened.

This series of events is not unlikely for a person with limited sexual knowledge and judgment, lack of assertiveness skills, low self-esteem and a strong desire to please. What can be done to help prevent such occurrences?

In applying *In Defense of Ourselves* to developmentally disabled women, several preliminary steps must be taken. Initially, there must be effective teaching of basic sexual knowledge along with an understanding of the meaning of sex within a relationship. A woman must understand that she can *choose* to have sex, and that if she does not choose it, then it is rape, and that is a crime. To promote this kind of understanding, use of concrete examples and a straightforward behavioral approach† in a group or individual setting is recommended. For example, use of specific situations as case examples for teaching might be useful in helping a developmentally disabled woman differentiate between rape and consenting sex. Modeling of openness and comfort by the parent, teacher or counselor while discussing sex is also very important.

Along with presentations of factual information, development of the key characteristics of assertiveness and self-esteem is essential. Some of the behavioral exercises or "First Thoughts" would be very beneficial to self-esteem development, such as structured repetition of positive statements about selves and receiving of positive feedback from others. Behavioral rehearsal, as seen from my experience, is the most efficient method for changing attitudes and behavior of people who have difficulty intellectualizing and conceptualizing about abstract concepts such as assertiveness and self-esteem. These techniques, as described in this book, could be utilized in group settings, or individual counseling and between parents and daughters.

Body language is frequently an obvious but ignored symbol of how one feels about one's own worth. Actual behavioral practicing of walking, standing, etc., in front of mirrors and/or using videotape could facilitate development of confident body posture and thus lead to increased self-esteem and greater body-image acceptance. Along with body language, tone of voice is another area in which developmentally disabled women could gain some confidence. Actual behavioral practicing of confident speech and yelling for help when necessary could be practiced using audio tape for feedback.

It appears that all of these behavioral exercises could be implemented in a group setting using feedback from group leaders, each other, video and audio tape to help developmentally disabled women combine the practiced skills into an over-all increased sense of self-confidence and self-esteem. With developmentally disabled women, it would probably be more effective to begin with body language and tone of voice exercises before including the self-esteem exercises.

Concurrently, increased assertiveness skills are needed and seem to go hand in hand with self-esteem; when one is developed, the other is likely to increase also. In doing assertiveness training with developmentally disabled women, I have found it very difficult to convey an actual understanding of what it is and what are its benefits. I have found a strong moral resistance to the idea that one has the right to hurt someone else's feeling, even if that person is infringing inappropriately in one's space. For example, one woman had great difficulty asking an intrusive neighbor to leave her apartment and turning down requests from the neighbor to do things she did not really want to do. Although the woman did not feel she could come right out and state her true feelings, she engaged in various

† A behavioral approach usually consists of *doing*, i.e., practicing behaviors, role-plays, giving and receiving of positive feedback, as opposed to *talking* or *intellectualizing* about why we are teaching a certain concept.

forms of passive/aggressive resistance to deal with her neighbor. For instance, she would pretend not to be home, or lie to her neighbor in a nice tone of voice, but talk about her in very negative tones behind her back. Another woman could see no difference between telling a co-worker it bothers her when he swears (using an "I" message), and telling him to stop swearing ("you" message). Religious attitudes seem to play a part in the resistance to believing in the right to be assertive. Some religious teachings might be interpreted to mean that one must always place the interests of others above one's own needs. A person who believes this may find it hard to accept that it is her right to be assertive. Many developmentally disabled women also seem to gain their greatest sense of self-worth from being a "nice" person since other worthwhile roles, such as that of "productive worker" or "successful student," have not been left open to them. All of this seems to tie in with the "American Etiquette" and proper behavior women have been trained to engage in, and makes it doubly difficult to train assertiveness.

However, in focusing on rape prevention, a relatively small range of assertiveness skills could help a developmentally disabled woman avoid a rape situation. She must first know what is rape and what is not rape, and learn to say *no* when she does not want sexual contact at whatever the level of contact may be. Repeated and frequent behavioral rehearsals of saying no in various role-played potentially dangerous situations might help a woman learn to feel more comfortable saying no.

This also leads us back again to the importance of believing that "I am *worth* defending," which, in turn, leads to the topic of self-defense. Some developmentally disabled women would be capable of physically defending themselves and others might have great difficulty doing so, just as is the case with all women. In teaching self-defense to developmentally disabled women, focusing on two or three basic techniques, such as the stompkick, palm-heel strike to the nose and the groin pull, would probably be more useful than risking confusion by bringing up numerous techniques for numerous assault situations. Use of these techniques *only* in actual clear assault situations must be stressed. I would recommend avoiding discussion or training in self-defense until you are sure the women know what constitutes an assault situation and show enough self-confidence to put these techniques into practice without hesitation. Otherwise, a panic reaction might occur, leading to greater paranoia and overreaction rather than increased confidence in one's self-defense skills. I know of no cases of physical self-defense training thus far with developmentally disabled women, and would use caution in attempting it. Much time spent in developing self-esteem, assertiveness and appropriate use of self-defense techniques will probably be necessary before readiness for actual self-defense training is reached. Also, some mention of the variable of the rapist with a weapon must be made in teaching self-defense. This is one area the book did not seem to cover.

I have not addressed myself to women with physical handicaps. The sections of this book dealing with assertiveness and our social conditioning is valid for physically disabled women. The self-defense portion would need to be greatly adapted for that population. An entirely separate treatment of self-defense for physically disabled women is in order.

To summarize, it seems that many of the concepts and techniques presented in *In Defense of Ourselves* apply quite directly to developmentally disabled women. Modifications of the concepts to a teaching process based on explicit and clear information. Behavioral techniques are additionally recommended. This is as opposed to a rap group or insight-oriented approach to teaching sexuality awareness, assertiveness and self-esteem development. These concepts are doubly important for developmentally disabled women to develop because, as pointed out earlier, they frequently have even greater needs in these areas, and are thus more prone to allow a potentially assaultive situation become a full-blown rape. The unique approach of *In Defense of Ourselves* to rape prevention for all women is greatly appreciated. It helps me to understand much more clearly how my own personality dynamics can influence my response in a rape situation, and how I can develop more control over what happens to my body. This in itself is a beginning toward greater confidence. Professionally, I now have a clearer direction to follow in implementing programs to actually help developmentally disabled women prevent rape.

Notes

1 George Gerbner. "Violence in Television Drama: Trends and Symbolic Functions," *Television and Social Behavior*. Washington, D.C.: U. S. Government Printing Office, 1972, pp. 28–187.

2 United Methodist Women's Television Monitoring Project, *Sex Role Stereotyping in Prime Time Television*. New York: 47 Riverside Drive, 1976.

3 Ibid.

4 Muriel Cantor. "Women in Public Broadcasting," *Journal of Communications*, 27 (1), 1977, pp. 14–19.

5 National Organization for Women, *A Study of Newspapers in the Washington, D.C./ Surburban Area*. Northern Virginia NOW, 1973.

6 Susan Miller. "The Content of News Photos: Women's and Men's Roles," *Journalism Quarterly*, Vol. 52, No. 1, Spring 1976, pp. 70–75.

7 James Culley, and Rex Bennett. "Selling Women, Selling Blacks," *Journal of Communications*, 26 (4), 1976, pp. 160–74.

8 Linda Busby. "Sex Role Research on the Mass Media," *Journal of Communications*, 25 (4), 1975, pp. 107–31.

9 Matilda Butler, and William Paisley. *The Flawed Mirror: Women and the Mass Media*. Washington, D.C.: Communications Press, 1977, Chap. 6.

10 Lee Israel. "Women in Film: Saving an Endangered Species." *MS.* magazine, February 1975, p. 28.

11 Joan Mellen. *Women and Their Sexuality in the New Films*. New York: Horizon Press, 1973, pp. 12, 24, 29.

12 Caroline Isber, and Muriel Cantor. *Report of the Task Force on Women and Public Broadcasting*. Corporation for Public Broadcasting, 1111 16th Street N.W., Washington, D.C. 20036, 1975.

13 Linda Busby. "Defining the Sex-role Standard in Commercial Network Television Programs Directed Toward Children," *Journalism Quarterly*, 51 (4), Winter 1974, pp. 690–96.

14 Inge K. Broverman, Donald M. Broverman, Frank E. Clarkson, Paul S. Rosenkrantz, and Susan R. Vogel. "Sex-role Stereotypes and Clinical Judgments of Mental Health," *Journal of Consulting and Clinical Psychology*, 34:1, 1970, pp. 1–7.

15 Martin E. P. Seligman. "Fall Into Helplessness," *Psychology Today*, June 1973, pp. 43–47.